Cooking with Crab

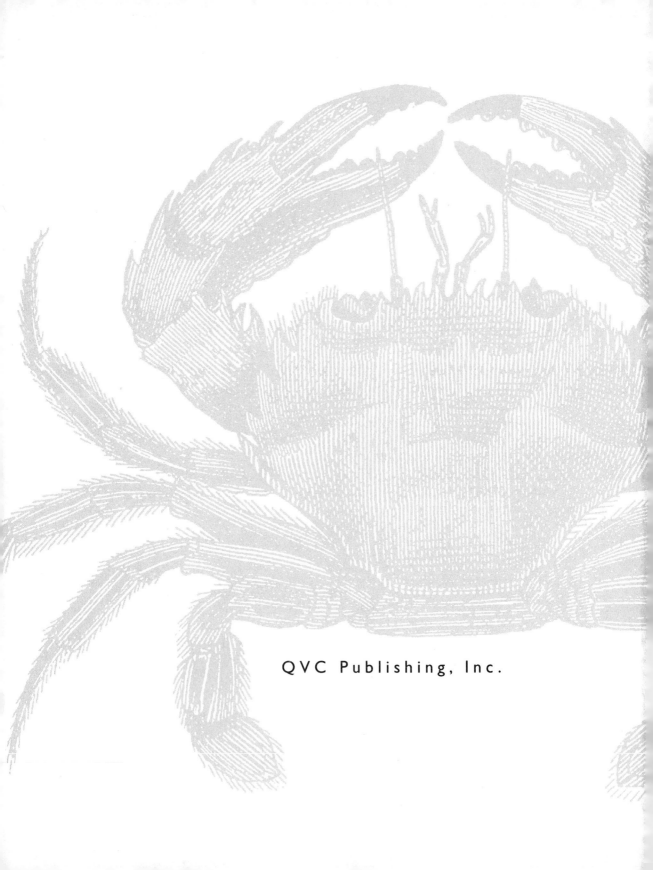

QVC Publishing, Inc.

Cooking with Crab

BEST-LOVED RECIPES AND MENUS FROM

Chesapeake Bay Gourmet

MARGIE KAUFFMAN

QVC Publishing, Inc.
Jill Cohen, Vice President and Publisher
Ellen Bruzelius, General Manager
Sarah Butterworth, Editorial Director
Cassandra Reynolds, Executive Assistant

Produced in association with Patrick Filley Associates, Inc.
Book design by Marjorie Anderson

Photography by Mark Thomas Studio

Prop styling by Nancy Micklin

Food Styling by Bobbi Cappelli

Original illustrations by Kristina Lang

Q Publishing and colophon are trademarks of QVC Publishing, Inc.

Published by QVC Publishing, Inc.,
50 Main Street, Mt. Kisco, New York 10549

Manufactured in Hong Kong

ISBN: 1-928-99833-X

First Edition

10 9 8 7 6 5 4 3 2 1

QVC Publishing books are available at special discounts when purchased in
bulk for premiums and sales promotions as well as for fund-raising or
educational use. Special editions or book excerpts can be created to
specification. For details, contact the address above.

Table of Contents

Introduction

I THINK YOU'D HAVE TO SAY, THE WATER IS IN OUR BLOOD. There were all those endless summer days of childhood spent on Bird River, an arm of the Chesapeake Bay, right at the end of our neighborhood in Baltimore. How could it not be? It was so close, all of our activities and so much pleasure focused on the river.

As soon as the water warmed up in the spring, we'd head to the backyard and dig for fishing worms, and some of my fondest memories are of crabbing with my brother Les in a little rowboat. I'd have to go along to keep an eye on him because I was the older sister. We'd float in sunshine on sparkling water, going out at different times of day so Les could check his trotline, a method Chesapeake watermen have used to catch crab since the 19th century. We used empty milk jugs for floats along the line and had cinder block anchors at each end. Salted eel was our bait, bought at the dock store. Gently and quietly pulling up the line hand over hand to check the bait tied at intervals, we'd carefully reach out with a net to scoop in an unsuspecting crab—a true feat with these feisty creatures who let go at the slightest hint of foul play. Usually successful, with great glee we'd take our wiggling catch home to be cooked by Mother.

Our little corner on Bird River is but one part of the magnificent Chesapeake Bay. This remarkable estuary is the largest in North America. It stretches across Maryland, Delaware and Virginia, some 200 miles in length, and has more than 4,600 miles of shoreline, rivers, creeks, tidal flats, wetlands and marshes. Formed when the last great ice sheet melted from North America, its watershed begins with the Susquehanna River in Cooperstown, New York. As the mighty Susquehanna travels south to empty into the Chesapeake Bay, it is joined by numerous other tributaries that flow from the Allegheny Mountains, the eastern slope of the ancient, rocky Appalachian rib that runs north and south on the eastern side of the continent. This network of rivers and streams ultimately encompasses 64,000 square miles in four more states.

The eastern seaboard's southern swath of cities, from Baltimore and Washington, D.C., to Norfolk, Virginia, along with all the residents living around the Bay, today account for more than 8,000,000 people. The skyscrapers of these metropolitan areas contrast with rolling hills, cliffs and forests that also make up the landscape on the Chesapeake's western shore. Its eastern shore is completely different with flat, wide open farmland and orchards, charming fishing villages and summer communities. To the south, expansive marshes and wetlands are breeding grounds for a myriad species of wildlife, waterfowl and sea creatures, including the famed Atlantic blue crab.

As fresh water rivers mingle with tide waters amid the plains and marshes of the Chesapeake, they create an amazingly fertile environment for fish and shellfish. From briny Chincoteague oysters and Rockfish to its abundant clams and the sweet Atlantic blue crab, the list of the Bay's delicious native bounty is long—and has been happily feasted on by humans for centuries. It's no wonder Native Americans of the Susquehannock tribe named the waterway "Chesapeake," which translated means "Great Shellfish Bay."

The Chesapeake Bay was home to prosperous Native American tribes and its bounty of constant and sustainable foods enabled them to thrive. No doubt this food supply contributed as well to the success of the first colonial outposts in the New World. English captain John L. Smith and a small party of white settlers established Jamestown, Virginia, in 1607, quickly discovering the area's abundant natural food supply. More settlers followed and the Chesapeake, along with New England, quickly became a commercial hub for the Colonies.

Because of this early development, the Chesapeake Bay is intimately linked with events in American history. The Potomac River was the site of several key Revolutionary War events, and today connects the nation's capital, Washington, D.C., with the sea. Frances Scott Key wrote our national anthem "The Star Spangled Banner" when Fort McHenry in the Baltimore harbor was being bombarded during a battle in the War of 1812.

With such a bounty of unique native foods right at their doorstep, so to speak, Chesapeake Bay cooks naturally developed their own cooking style and traditions, a style that takes honors as one of America's oldest regional cuisines. While one pot cooking was the norm in the 1700s, when a soup, stew or casserole could be made easily over an open fire using venison, ham, fish, seafood or chicken, it works for today's busy cooks, too.

Enhancing the culinary traditions of our forebears are those of our modern kitchens and dining tables, along with the ethnic dishes we've adopted from our region's immigrants. You may not know that Baltimore was the second largest port of entry on the East Coast for European immigrants in the mid to late 1880s. German immigrants brought native dishes like spare ribs and sauerkraut with them. In fact, sauerkraut served with roast turkey at Thanksgiving is a particularly unique tradition in Baltimore. We have to have it! French and English immigrants gave us soups, bisques and soufflés. Gumbos and Creole dishes come from our African-American ancestors.

Seasonal cooking has always been at the heart of Chesapeake Bay cuisine; we live close to the source of our regional food and have learned to honor its cycles. Now, farmer's markets are springing up in more places, making it easier than ever to enjoy the area's abundance of fresh, locally grown produce like corn, vine-ripened tomatoes, blackberries, strawberries, apples and local specialties like Smithfield country ham and sausage.

But if you ask anyone who lives here what our most famous regional dish is, the instant answer will be crab. Prized for its succulent meat, the Latin name of the Atlantic blue crab is *Callinectes sapidus,* which means "savory beautiful swimmer."

This feisty crustacean actually resides up and down the Atlantic coastline from Maine to Florida and into the Gulf of Mexico. Its favorite habitat, however, is the Chesapeake Bay where the ebb and flow of fresh and salt waters, the lush marsh grass and countless coves and inlets, provide ideal living conditions for a thriving blue crab population. Despite environmental pressures—the population living around the Chesapeake Bay has increased more than 50 percent since the 1950s, meaning less crab habitat and more people interested in eating them—the blue crab is so far holding its own and maintaining its population. The happy result is the world's oldest and largest commercial crab fishery.

For generations, industrious Chesapeake Bay watermen have made a living by harvesting the Atlantic blue crab. From late April or right around Memorial Day, until October or November, depending on the weather, these hardy watermen ply their trade using long trotlines, multibaited at intervals and running along the floor of the Bay, or traps and crab pots, which a crab can walk into as they meander in search of food, but never out of.

Watermen have a language all their own for the blue crab, colorful names that are familiar to anyone who has grown up on the Chesapeake. While a visitor will raise their eyebrows to hear names like "jimmy," "sook," and "peeler," discussed on the docks, a waterman would know exactly what these words mean and what sex or stage of a crab's life was being discussed. For example, most crabs caught are "jimmies," male crabs that are best steamed. They are distinguished from female crabs by having an inverted "T" on their underside. Females, called "sooks," have a fuller, more rounded underside and can be distinguished by their red claws. Sooks generally are steamed and their meat sold as one of four grades of crabmeat.

The life cycle of the Atlantic blue crab gives us several delicious eating opportunities. Every blue crab undergoes a molting process as it grows, a process which requires it to shed its hard shell 20 to 23 times during its three-year life span. When a blue crab backs out of its shell during one of these molting phases, it's a soft-shell crab. Watermen watch "peeler" crabs closely, paying attention to marks on their legs and body, looking for clues as to exactly when a crab will shed its shell and become a soft-shell crab. Removed from the water, the soft crab's shell stops rehardening and it's quickly shipped off to meet its fate as a prized delicacy on some dining table.

Crabs also inspired one of our beloved Chesapeake Bay social rituals, the backyard crab feast. To gather crabs for this event, it's great fun to try your hand at crabbing. Anyone can do it, from a dock, a bridge or off a pier, and then bring the loot home to share with a delighted crowd of friends and family. You can also try "scapping" or baitless crabbing where you take a crab net and simply scoop crabs into it. To be successful with this method, you'll have to talk with locals to see where crabs gather and then consult a tide table before walking into the water to find crabs. Remember that crabs can see you as soon as you see them!

It's unlikely that your crabbing expedition will fail, but have no worries, it's always possible during crab season to buy live or cooked crabs, or even fresh crabmeat already picked. Sometimes it's necessary to do this to save time and focus on the real reason for a crab feast. Because the true sport of a traditional Chesapeake Bay crab feast is to gather a group of family and friends together on a hot, steamy summer night in the backyard or on the deck around tables laden with platters of hot, steamed crabs and totally indulge everyone's crab passions with this prized treat. It's a messy job to pick apart a steamed crab, but it seems to guarantee good humor. Not to mention that there are delicious side dishes to eat when you need a break from crab. Or at least that's how it works in my family.

Lots of locals like to avoid the clean-up after a outdoor bash, so they head instead for their favorite crab house. These can be simple, down-home neighborhood restaurants, or a fancy dinner spot, but they're always filled with a good-natured crowd. The best spots have tables covered with newspaper or heavy brown paper. You'll want to roll up your sleeves and prepare to get messy to snare those succulent bites of steamed crab. Crab-picking skills are developed with patience and practice, or inherited if you're a Chesapeake Bay native.

Since the Chesapeake Bay lifestyle with all its warm traditions, soaks into your soul, I wasn't surprised when my brother and sister-in-law established M&I Seafood 20 years ago to sell handmade frozen crab cakes to grocery chains in the Baltimore area. They were doing what comes naturally and had found a niche no one else was filling.

When my husband and I became involved with M&I Seafood some years later, we tapped our shared restaurant management experience (at Gino's fast food chain in Baltimore) to run the company. Each of us brought experiences and strengths to the company that have been channeled into specific areas of responsibility. Linda (Les's wife) manages our front office and reception, Les buys our crabmeat, my husband Ron is involved with sales, marketing and financial matters, and I manage the day-to-day operation of the company. Our sons are now also involved in various areas of the business.

Over the years, our business evolved and we supplied several wholesale club retailers in the area, as well as area grocery chains. In 1987, we almost sold the business when I was diagnosed with thyroid cancer. But when that deal fell through and I recovered from surgery, we reassessed our goals and decided to get involved full-time again. We became even fiercer about making the company a success since we had already put so much into it.

We knew that to make our business grow, we'd have to find new outlets, especially for our high-end products. In 1994, we started Chesapeake Bay Gourmet, our mail-order business featuring our new 100 percent jumbo lump gourmet crab cakes and other top-of-the-line seafood products like crab en croute and lobster cakes. We attended several fancy food shows to introduce our gourmet line. With mail order, our challenge was to fulfill orders quickly and master the art of shipping to maintain our signature quality. Need I say that we got to be very good friends with our UPS man, and our Styrofoam and dry ice suppliers?

The real turning point for our business came in 1995, on Sunday, October 22, 1995, to be exact. Earlier that summer in July we had received an invitation from the Maryland Department of Business and Economic Development to submit a product for consideration for QVC's nationwide new product search called "The Quest for America's Best." The televised shopping channel was visiting 50 states in 50 weeks to find small vendors with regional products to feature on the show. We lived on Kent Island just over the bridge from

Baltimore and we didn't have cable on the island, so we'd never seen the show. Still, one of our employees encouraged us and we decided to "audition" our old-fashioned-all Jumbo Lump Crab Cakes for the taste test. I brought my own frying pan for that, and Ron had to find an extension cord to plug it in for the demonstration because our table was miles from the nearest outlet! To our great surprise, from this preview, we were one of 20 Maryland products selected to participate on QVC from among 200 products submitted.

The next step was to "go live" on television and present our crab cakes to a national audience. Much to my dismay, we were scheduled to appear first on the three-hour broadcast. Of course, we'd never appeared on television before, and now there was no one to watch to see the format or anticipate the host's questions. Even more daunting, we had under ten minutes to sell 2,000 dozen crab cakes! When we sat down after our ten minutes, someone whispered "sell-out" to me and I had to ask what that meant. On hearing, we were elated! But the excitement didn't last long faced with the challenge of packing and drop shipping crab cake orders for QVC customers all over the country. With a lot of help from our dedicated employees and two long ten-hour days, we made it.

Now when we appear on QVC, it's often for a one-hour program called "Chesapeake Bay Gourmet" which premiered in 1998 and usually features seven specialty food products. We may also be on for just ten minutes to present a single product, sometimes in the context of a QVC cooking show. We've become camera-savvy and learned to field call-in questions from listeners, as well as offer suggestions for product preparation and recipes.

Looking back on the past five years, we would all say it has been an amazing experience, and, of course, Chesapeake Bay Gourmet sales have taken off. In February 2000, we celebrated sales of 3,000,000 Jumbo Lump Crab Cakes sold to QVC customers. Our company has grown from eight people to 62, with 60 percent of our employees having between two and 17 years of service. It's a real family affair with sisters, brothers and mothers working together. This spring we moved into larger warehouse facilities in Baltimore to accommodate our production and sales increases. We're still family-owned and we firmly believe that no one is going to care about this business as much as we do or maintain its high standards.

All of this good fortune we ascribe to this beautiful and bountiful place where we are blessed to live. The Chesapeake Bay gave us our roots and our values. We are grateful that it has given us our livelihood as well.

If You Love Crab Cakes ...

AFTER 140 YEARS as the most acclaimed and succulent part of Chesapeake Bay cuisine, you would think a single, perfect crab cake recipe would exist in every family's kitchen along the shores of this 200-mile-long Bay. Not so. The search for the perfect crab cake is a fierce topic of discussion, debate and even, on occasion, fist fights, in this part of the world that I predict will rage on far into the 21st Century. We are simply too passionate about our region's signature dish to quietly and calmly agree on one basic recipe.

It's certain the first crab cakes were made by the women of native Chesapeake Bay Indian tribes. How could they resist, living on such bountiful shores? They taught early European settlers how to make their local delicacy, a mix of Atlantic blue crab with ingredients like herbs, vegetables and corn meal, formed into small, palm-sized flat cakes that were fried in hot bear fat. The rest, as they say, is history.

But as so often happens in culinary history, each region of the Chesapeake developed its own traditional style of crab cakes. And folks in each area are convinced their version is the absolute best! On the Eastern Shore, simple is preferred. Tender lumps of fresh-cooked crab are moistened only with lemon butter and formed into cakes before they are gently broiled.

Around Baltimore, where we hail from, we like some seasoning with our crab. You'll frequently find crab cakes in this area flavored with a slightly spicy, mayonnaise-enhanced batter and a bread or cracker binding. They can be either fried or broiled, although I remember my mother always pan frying them, as I do now.

In the southern part of our beautiful Bay, crab cakes become a tad exotic (to some) and a lightly seasoned cream sauce is used as the binder. These cakes are chilled to hold them together, lightly coated in bread crumbs, and then fried.

Knowing about all these different variations, it's easier to understand why, before M & I Seafood even began, it took my brother Les months to find and perfect what he thought was the perfect crab cake -- to a Baltimore native's taste buds. Les began his quest in 1980 when crab cakes were "hot" and just being discovered by chefs newly fascinated with American regional cooking. He realized that no one was selling frozen crab cakes in the area and that there could be a sizable market with grocery stores. He and other family members tested hundreds of crab cakes in their own kitchens, using recipes handed down from generations of Chesapeake Bay watermen, before they were satisfied they had the ultimate, most delicious combination of ingredients.

While these crab cakes were a terrific fit for M&I Seafood's grocery chain customers, we gradually realized that for the business to grow we needed other avenues to sell and market our products. We decided to develop a gourmet line of food products featuring our gourmet crab cakes, to reach new outlets. We'd tested several "upscale" recipes during Les's original search, but knew we'd have to come up with something very special to convince people to buy our gourmet crab cakes a second and third time.

So I took the best recipe for crab cakes that we had and started by trial and error to "tweak" its ingredients. I felt very strongly that we should only use beautiful jumbo lump crabmeat in our best crab cake recipe and eliminate all other types, and the others agreed, especially after they'd seen and tasted the difference. Then we tested the recipe over and over again—even having our employees try it to get their reactions. They are always quick to give an honest opinion!

For what is now our top-selling Chesapeake Bay Gourmet Supreme Blend crab cakes—with over 3,000,000 sold just through QVC alone—we use a slightly different type of binding to hold the cakes together, something that's critical when you use only jumbo lump crabmeat. These magnificent crab cakes contain only the finest jumbo lump crabmeat, pasteurized eggs, soda cracker crumbs, mayonnaise, margarine, Worcestershire sauce, mustard, baking powder, our secret seasonings and minced parsley. None of our crab cakes are ever breaded. From the beginning, the recipe hasn't changed except for switching to low-fat mayonnaise and low-sodium Worcestershire sauce to honor health considerations.

To make our Chesapeake Bay Gourmet Supreme Blend crab cakes, every pound of crabmeat we use is examined by hand to remove any cartilage or shell normally left in by the crabmeat supplier. In fact, the only mechanical piece of equipment used in making our crab cakes is a huge blender that mixes all the ingredients together except the crab meat. We add the crab meat by hand to retain its integrity. Each cake is formed using an ice cream scoop, then cryogenically frozen with CO_2 at $-80°F$ to quickly lock in the fresh taste and homemade flavor. Every mail-or phone-order shipment of Chesapeake Bay Gourmet Crab

Cakes is shipped in an insulated, Styrofoam container with dry ice that will hold the product for 48 to 60 hours.

Which brings me to a discussion of the actual crabmeat that goes into making crab cakes—because it's the crabmeat that contributes the flavor and texture to a crab cake. Not only that, crabmeat is an excellent source of high-quality protein, vitamins and minerals, including phosphorus, zinc, copper, calcium and iron. It's also low in fat, especially saturated fat. Since different parts of an Atlantic blue crab contain its meat, each will have its own subtle taste variations. Crabmeat is sorted into four grades that relate to what part of the crab it comes from.

- Top-of-the-line is "jumbo lump" crabmeat, the large, white succulent chunks of completely cleaned, solid crabmeat taken from the main shell that are so prized for premium crab cakes, or for any fancy crab dish. You only get two pieces of jumbo lump per crab.

- "Backfin" crabmeat, as its name implies, is the white body meat taken from the backfin section of the crab. It will have some large lump pieces and some broken body meat with a few shell pieces, and it's also ideal for crab cakes, crab imperial or other crab dishes.

- The "special" grade refers to smaller, white "flake meat" from the entire body and center parts of the crab, as well as a minimum amount of backfin and jumbo lump. It always needs to be picked over carefully to remove any shell or cartilage. It's used in crab cakes, soups, casseroles and dips.

- "Claw meat" is slightly brownish with a somewhat sweeter taste that's delicious in soups, dips and chowders. It also makes an economical crab cake for large gatherings at churches or local fairs. You'll find it too, in crab cakes served by small coffee shops and neighborhood taverns.

Most home cooks also combine different grades of crabmeat, and (obviously perhaps), all crabmeat is cooked before it is used in any recipe. Crabmeat can be purchased fresh in your local market, or right at the shore where the crabs are harvested—the ideal way for purists. Like any seafood, it's always best if you know your seafood merchant and he knows his suppliers.

In winter months when fresh crabmeat is not available, it's possible to buy pasteurized crabmeat. Pasteurized crabmeat, processed by a special heat method that prevents spoiling, is comparable to fresh. If left unopened, pasteurized crabmeat will keep for several months at 33°F to 35°F.

Also, note that crabmeat can be used interchangeably in a recipe, regardless of its source (Alaska, Gulf Coast, Florida), although we like to think our Chesapeake blues are vastly superior. If you're buying crabmeat to make crab cakes, plan on buying one pound to make eight crab cakes, enough for four people to have two cakes apiece.

Once you have your crabmeat, be sure to pick through it carefully to eliminate any small pieces of shell or cartilage. These pieces are always there, so take the time to comb through the meat and discard any shell or cartilage. Also, be careful not to break the beautiful, large lumps of crabmeat.

As I mentioned earlier, every crab cake needs a binding to hold the crabmeat together. A blend of wet ingredients and seasonings, a binding can include mayonnaise, eggs, cream or cream sauces, bread, cracker crumbs or bread cubes, and dry seasonings. The challenge is to find a perfect proportion of these ingredients that require a minimal amount of breading to hold the crabmeat together—and tastes delicious!

Seasonings are an integral part of the binder. They give every crab cake its personality. Seasonings can range from simple lemon juice and mustard, to minced parsley and prepared horseradish, or they can be lively additions like hot pepper sauces such as Tabasco or Worcestershire sauce. Every crab cake binder must also have its dash of our beloved regional Chesapeake seasonings like Old Bay and JO.

To make crab cakes, first separate the crab into its own bowl, and then mix together all the binding ingredients in another bowl. Next, sprinkle the breading (cracker or breadcrumbs) over the crabmeat, and then pour the binding mixture over the crabmeat. Gently and carefully toss all the ingredients with a rubber spatula or your hands, taking care not to break up the crabmeat.

Now to form the crab cakes. While some home cooks like ice cream scoops to make the individual cakes, you can also keep it simple and use your hands. Or place some of the crabmeat mixture into small rounded cups and invert those. Then, lightly press down on the mixture, flattening each cake so it's about one-inch thick. Whatever method you use, it's important to be gentle when forming the cakes. They should be held together loosely and not be too compacted. Size will depend on your preference, but don't fret if they vary slightly. Once the crab cakes are made, many cooks like to chill them in the refrigerator for an hour or so. This allows the binding to absorb more moisture so that the cakes hold together better while they're cooking.

Crab cakes can be cooked in several different ways as described below. You may enjoy experimenting with one or more methods to decide which you like best. The goal of any method is to produce a crab cake that's lightly browned on the outside, and soft and moist on the inside.

- **Sautéing:** This is the traditional cooking method in most Chesapeake Bay regions. In a heavy skillet, heat $1/4$-inch of olive oil until it's hot, but not smoking. Place the crab cakes gently into the oil, being careful not to crowd them. Sauté them for three to five minutes or until the edges begin to brown. Turn each one over with a wide spatula and brown on the other side for another three to five minutes. Remove the cooked crab cakes from the pan and drain on some paper towels. Keep them warm in a closed oven until all the crab cakes are sautéed and drained.

- **Deep-frying:** Place a large pot of vegetable oil over high heat and bring to 375°F. Then carefully place the crab cakes into the hot oil. Cook only a few crab cakes at a time so that the temperature of the oil doesn't lower too much. Note that the crab cakes will foam violently and want to float, so place a wire basket over the top of the oil to keep them submerged. The crab cakes are cooked when they stop bubbling, in about three to four minutes. They will not be very brown, but rather a light tan color. Remove the cakes from the oil using a wire skimmer or slotted spoon and place on paper towels to drain. Keep them warm in a closed oven until ready to serve.

- **Broiling:** Place the crab cakes on a lightly oiled baking sheet. Place the baking sheet four to five inches under the broiler flame and cook the crab cakes for four to five minutes or until the tops are nicely browned. Turn the cakes over and brown on the other side. Once the second side is browned, turn off the broiler, close the oven door and leave the crab cakes in the hot oven another five minutes before serving.

●**Grilling:** Bring a charcoal grill to a temperature where you can hold your hand just above the grill for two to three seconds. If the grill feels too hot, allow it to cool before cooking the crab cakes. Coat a metal cooling rack with vegetable spray. When the grill's heat is correct, place the crab cakes on the cooling rack and put this on the barbecue so that the barbecue's grill-work and the cooling rack's ribs are perpendicular. This will prevent the crab cakes from falling through the grate into the coals. Cook the crab cakes for five to seven minutes and then carefully turn them to cook five more minutes on the other side. Test the crab cakes with a fork. If they are still very loose or soft, lower the lid of the barbecue and cook three to five more minutes. Serve the crab cakes immediately.

● **Baking:** Preheat the oven to 350°F. Place on a baking pan, at least two inches apart. Cover the pan with foil and bake in the oven for 25 to 30 minutes. Remove and serve immediately.

In the Chesapeake Bay region, we rarely eat crab cakes by themselves. In fact, there is considerable discussion about exactly what makes the best condiment or sauce to serve with them, and what side dishes to serve, as well. As you'd expect, fresh lemon wedges and tartar sauce are naturals that "let the crab do the talking," but the list divides after that depending on where you are and who you're asking. Suggestions of what's best can range from a classic French rémoulade to updated accompaniments like my Roasted Red Pepper Sauce or even the zesty Black Bean Salsa. If you're serving crab cakes for breakfast or brunch in an inventive dish like Crab Cake Benedict, pair it with my Fruit salsa. Crab cakes are wonderful partners with any number of flavors, so that sauces can easily range from the traditional to the inventive.

Of course, sauces aren't the only thing eaten with crab cakes. We have what is called "time-out food," typical fare that's served at a crab feast when you want a break from all the crab picking, but which goes equally well with crab cakes. Heaping platters of piping hot French fries and trenches of coleslaw are standard side dishes at restaurants. Depending on the season, there might also be bowls of potato salad, platters of corn on the cob, sliced ripe tomatoes and crisp new asparagus, not to mention those perennial southern favorites, biscuits and corn bread. We know our food in this part of the country and we love to eat!

With all the delicious pleasure crab cakes bring to those of us living around the Chesapeake Bay—and to those of you visiting or now sharing our bounty courtesy of QVC and air freight deliveries—it's guaranteed that this shining star of our regional fare will never lose its appeal.

No-Fat Crab Cakes

Dieters, you can have your crab cakes and eat them, too. Nonfat mayonnaise cuts calories and fat, but still allows that magic proportion of binding ingredients and seasonings that every crab cake recipe strives for. This version is so good no one will guess they're no-fat.

¾ cup cracker crumbs

¾ cup breadcrumbs

½ teaspoon Chesapeake seasoning (such as Old Bay or JO)

¼ teaspoon salt

¼ teaspoon freshly ground pepper

2 egg whites

2 teaspoons chopped fresh parsley

1 tablespoon minced green onions

¼ cup nonfat mayonnaise

1 teaspoon Worcestershire sauce

1 tablespoon Dijon-style mustard

2 tablespoons water

½ pound lump crabmeat, drained, picked over

3 tablespoons olive oil

In a small mixing bowl, combine the cracker crumbs, breadcrumbs, Chesapeake seasoning, salt and pepper. In a medium-size bowl, whisk together the egg whites, parsley, green onions, mayonnaise, Worcestershire sauce, mustard and water. Stir the dry ingredients into the wet and when well combined, gently fold in the crabmeat. Shape the mixture into 6 tight balls and refrigerate for 1 hour.

In a large, heavy skillet over medium-high heat, heat the oil until hot but not smoking. Flatten the crab balls to about a 1-inch thickness and add to the frying pan, being sure not to crowd the pan. Cook 6 minutes on each side. Remove and drain on a stack of paper towels. Serve immediately.

makes about 6 crab cakes

M E N U

Crab Cake Benedict • 21

Roasted Red Bliss Potatoes with Scallions

Minted Peas

Fresh Fruit

Crab Cake Benedict

Crab cakes for breakfast or brunch? Yes! We invented this delicious pairing of eggs Benedict with crab cakes and it's an elegant dish that's perfect for entertaining or just for a lazy weekend morning. You'll find the tropical fruit salsa is a delightful accent to the crab cakes.

3   egg yolks

Juice of 1 lemon

½   teaspoon salt

1   cup unsalted butter, softened

2   4-ounce crab cakes

1   tablespoon white vinegar

2   eggs

2   English muffins

1   tablespoon capers

Place a small, heatproof bowl over a pot of steaming water. Add the egg yolks, lemon juice and salt. Using a wire whisk, beat the butter, a tablespoon at a time, into the yolk mixture. You might need to remove the bowl from the steam from time to time. When all the butter is incorporated, remove from the heat and set aside.

Preheat the oven to 350°F. Place the crab cakes on a baking sheet and cook for 15 minutes.

Bring a small, nonstick pot of water to a simmer. Add the white vinegar and gently drop the eggs in the water. Do not allow the water to boil or the eggs will fall apart. Cook until the whites are opaque but the yolks are not.

While the eggs are poaching, toast the English muffins and then place them on the serving plates. Lift the cooked eggs out of the water with a slotted spoon. Allow all of the water to drain off before placing on the English muffins. Spoon some of the hollandaise sauce over the eggs and garnish with the capers.

Serve 1 egg Benedict along with 1 crab cake placed on the other half of the English muffin.

serves 2

Black Bean Salsa

Say "Olé!" to this crab cake condiment! South-of-the-border ingredients combine in a zesty salsa that adds some ethnic flair to Chesapeake Bay traditions.

¾ cup diced yellow onion

¾ cup diced red bell pepper

½ cup seeded diced tomato

1 tablespoon fresh lime juice

1 tablespoon white balsamic vinegar

1 tablespoon olive oil

2 teaspoons minced garlic

½ teaspoon salt

½ teaspoon ground cumin

1 15-ounce can black beans, drained, rinsed

2 tablespoons chopped fresh cilantro

1 tablespoon whole fresh thyme leaves

In a medium-size mixing bowl, combine all of the ingredients. Cover with plastic wrap and chill for 2 hours.

makes 1 pint

Traditional Tartar Sauce

Out-of-towners have introduced us to melted butter as a dipping sauce for crab cakes, but most Chesapeake Bay natives are faithful to traditional tartar sauce. The secret tang in my version comes from the dash of Dijon-style mustard.

¾ cup mayonnaise

3 green onions, sliced

1 tablespoon chopped fresh parsley

1 tablespoon chopped fresh tarragon

¼ cup minced gherkins

1 tablespoon chopped capers

2 teaspoons Dijon-style mustard

1 teaspoon sugar

¼ teaspoon salt

½ teaspoon freshly ground pepper

2 tablespoons red wine vinegar

In a small mixing bowl, using a wire whisk, place all of the ingredients and stir until combined. Cover with plastic wrap and chill for at least 2 hours.

serves 4

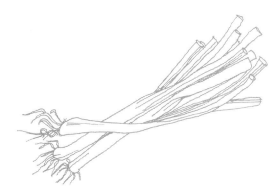

Creamy Horseradish Sauce

- - -

6 tablespoons prepared horseradish

1 tablespoon Dijon-style mustard

½ cup sour cream

¼ cup mayonnaise

2 tablespoons chopped fresh chives

½ teaspoon salt

½ teaspoon freshly ground pepper

Place all of the ingredients in a small mixing bowl. Using a wire whisk, stir until combined well.

serves 4

Curry Sauce with Chutney

- - -

3 tablespoons unsalted butter

1 shallot, minced

1 tablespoon curry powder

1 teaspoon freshly ground pepper

1 teaspoon salt

1 cup sour cream

2 tablespoons chopped fresh cilantro

3 tablespoons mango chutney

In a medium-size, heavy skillet over medium-high heat, melt the butter. Add the shallot and sauté for 3 minutes. Add the curry powder and cook for another 5 minutes, stirring frequently. Add the pepper and salt and remove the skillet from the heat.

Using a wire whisk, stir in the sour cream until the mixture is smooth. With a rubber spatula, fold in the cilantro and then the chutney. Cover and chill for at least 2 hours.

serves 4

Chipotle Remoulade

A twist on the classic remoulade, I use chipotle peppers, which are dried or smoked jalapeño peppers. A little "fire" is exciting with the mellow, nutty flavor of Chesapeake Bay crab cakes. You can vary the heat to taste by adding more or less pepper.

½   cup sliced green onions

¼   cup chopped fresh parsley

2   tablespoons ketchup

1   tablespoon lemon juice

1   tablespoon Worcestershire sauce

1   tablespoon white vinegar

1   tablespoon yellow mustard

1   tablespoon minced garlic

1   canned chipotle pepper

1   tablespoon adobo sauce from canned chipotle peppers

1   teaspoon salt

½   cup mayonnaise

Combine the first 11 ingredients and process in a food processor until smooth.

Add the mayonnaise and process until blended. Serve with crab cakes.

makes 1¼ cups

MENU

• • •

Hot Spinach Dipping Sauce with Tortilla Chips • 43

Crab Cakes

For tasting:

Black Bean Salsa • 22

Chipotle Remoulade • 25

Roasted Red Pepper Sauce • 27

Fruit Salsa • 28

Giant Fruit Popover • 128

Roasted Red Pepper Sauce

Ask six locals what sauce goes best with crab cakes and you'll get six different answers. We're opinionated about our food here! My family loves this colorful, creamy dip that's a sophisticated alternative to traditional tartar sauce. It also makes an excellent pasta sauce.

4   red bell peppers, halved, deseeded

2   tablespoons olive oil

2   garlic cloves, minced

2   tablespoons Sherry

1   cup light cream

Salt and freshly ground pepper to taste

Turn the oven on to broil. Place the pepper halves on a baking sheet, skin side up, just under the flame. Broil until they char and blister, about 5 minutes. Remove from the oven and when they have cooled to the touch, peel off the skin. Chop coarsely.

Place the oil and garlic in a large, heavy skillet and heat over a medium flame. Sauté for 3 minutes and add the red peppers and Sherry. Bring to a boil, then reduce the heat and simmer for 10 minutes.

Place the contents of the skillet in a blender or food processor and puree. Add the cream and process until the sauce is well mixed. Return the sauce to the heat, adjust the flavor with salt and pepper and serve.

makes I pint

Fruit Salsa

Tropical fresh fruits provide the base for this sweet and sour salsa that's an unexpectedly flavorful counterpoint to crab cakes. You'll find it especially refreshing served with grilled crab cakes for a summer dinner.

¾ cup finely diced mango

¼ cup finely diced pineapple

2 tablespoons minced red onion

½ jalapeño pepper, seeded, finely diced

2 tablespoons chopped fresh cilantro

¼ teaspoon ground cumin

½ teaspoon salt

½ teaspoon freshly ground pepper

¼ cup olive oil

2 tablespoons fresh lime juice

In a small mixing bowl, combine all of the ingredients. Cover with plastic wrap and chill for 1 hour.

serves 4

Summer Corn Relish

Corn on the cob is one of those "time out" foods at a Chesapeake Bay crab fest, when you pause between rounds of crab picking and eat something else. If there is any leftover corn, I slice the kernels off the cobs for this relish. Or make it easy and use frozen corn.

1	strip bacon
2	tablespoons olive oil
1	tablespoon minced garlic
3	cups fresh corn kernels or frozen, thawed
1	red bell pepper
4	green onions
1	teaspoon salt
½	teaspoon freshly cracked pepper
2	tablespoons cider vinegar

In a large, heavy skillet over medium heat, fry the bacon until crisp. Place on a paper towel to drain. Add the oil to the skillet and sauté the garlic for 3 minutes. Add the corn kernels. Cut the pepper into small dice and slice the green onions. Add to the corn and sauté for 5 minutes, until the corn begins to brown. Remove to a medium bowl. Sprinkle with the salt, pepper and cider. Crumble the bacon over the relish and toss well.

serves 6

My Favorite Recipes

I LOVE TO COOK. I ALWAYS HAVE. Cooking for my family and friends is a source of great pleasure in my life. I cook to please people and I enjoy the applause and appreciation, but the real reward is in the fellowship that's created around the table when a delicious meal is shared. Fortunately I raised two boys, who, along with my husband Ron, would enthusiastically try almost anything I made. I followed the rule that my mother set and urged them to try something at least once (although I drew the line myself as a child and refused to take a single bite of canned asparagus). Often they were surprised at how much they liked something new.

The recipes collected here are my favorites, gathered from happy decades of cooking for a family as a working mother, cooking for special occasions and holidays, and cooking just for simple, everyday weeknight suppers. I've included recipes for appetizers, soups, stews and chowders, sauces and relishes, main dishes, sides, breads, and, of course, desserts. These are recipes for the home cook, which is what I consider myself, who needs a repertoire of simple, everyday meals made with seasonal ingredients, but also on occasion wants to spend a little extra time to make something more elaborate.

With this in mind, you'll find my tried and true recipes for famous Chesapeake Bay classics like Maryland Crab Soup Supreme, Fried Soft Crabs in Beer Batter, Bessie's Crab Pudding, Bacon Potato Salad, Crab Imperial with Smithfield Hamand Blueberry Shortcake. We take great pride in our culinary traditions that are inspired by the bounty of our great Bay and it's my pleasure to share these with you.

I've also included recipes that I've created or rely on over and over for relaxed weekend brunches for Ron and myself, or weekday suppers when we're home and hungry after a long day at Chesapeake Bay Gourmet. They are easy and fast to prepare, even from scratch, but have a bit of flair and lots of flavor. Try the delicious Pasta with Smoked Salmon and Lemon Crème Fraîche. For brunch I think you'll love the two dishes I created: Crab Cake Benedict and Crab, Cheese and Bacon Frittata. I didn't forget dessert in this group either. My Easy Apple Tart or Cold Lemon Dessert are a perfect sweet finish for a weekday supper.

When I'm cooking for a special occasion I shift gears completely and love to take the time to create a dish that will inspire ooh's and aah's from friends gathered for a dinner party. Tuna with Sautéed Spinach and Béarnaise Sauce always wins applause for its medley of flavors complementing the succulent fish. So does the dramatic Salmon in Puff Pastry with Thyme Butter or Lobster-Stuffed Tenderloin of Beef, both irresistible pairings of textures and flavors. I have some knockout desserts in the special occasion category as well. Crepe Napoleons with Apple Compote and Apple Caramel Sauce is a wonderful finale to any autumn dinner and well worth the effort to make, as is the decadent Toasted Hazelnut Chocolate Marquise with its luscious chocolate filling.

As you can tell, my list of favorite recipes is long and diverse. It's grounded in old-fashioned dishes representing the Chesapeake Bay's traditional ingredients and cooking style, as well as complemented by tantalizing new pairings that reflect our adventuresome modern tastebuds. Whichever recipes here inspire and entice you into the kitchen, I hope they bring you and your family and friends as much pleasure as they have me.

STARTERS

Hot Crab Dip

This easy-to-make appetizer always wins raves from my guests. Its nutty crab flavor in a smooth spread contrasts pleasantly with crisp wheat crackers or melba toast rounds. Reserve some to serve with bagels the next morning and you'll earn even more applause.

2   8-ounce packages cream cheese, softened

½   cup sour cream

½   cup milk

3   tablespoons mayonnaise

2   tablespoons lemon juice

1   tablespoon Worcestershire sauce

1½   teaspoons dry mustard

Pinch garlic salt

½   cup grated Cheddar cheese

½   pound backfin crabmeat, drained, picked over

Paprika

½   teaspoon Chesapeake seasoning (such as Old Bay or JO)

In a large mixing bowl, working with a wire whisk, combine the cream cheese, sour cream, milk, mayonnaise, lemon juice, Worcestershire sauce, mustard and garlic salt. Whisk until creamy and smooth. Stir in 2 tablespoons of grated cheese. With a rubber spatula, fold in the crabmeat.

Preheat the oven to 350°F. Grease a 10-cup casserole. Pour in the crab mixture. Top with the remaining cheese. Sprinkle with the paprika and Chesapeake seasoning. Bake for 30 minutes, until the dip is bubbly and slightly browned.

makes 4 cups

Mother's Deviled Crab

My mother probably learned to make this in the 1920s when it was all the rage on the East Coast. The name comes from the cooking process that combines a food with hot, spicy seasonings. Served in a crab's top shell or a large scallop shell, it's still a dramatic dish.

3   tablespoons unsalted butter

3   tablespoons flour

1   cup milk

10 to 12 decorative ovenproof shells

Butter for coating shells

1   egg

1   tablespoon Worcestershire sauce

1   teaspoon prepared mustard

1   teaspoon lemon juice

½   teaspoon celery seed

Dash hot pepper sauce (such as Tabasco)

¼   teaspoon salt

⅛   teaspoon freshly ground pepper

1   pound lump crabmeat, drained, picked over

In a small, heavy saucepot over low heat, melt the butter. Add the flour and stir until a paste is formed. Cook for 3 to 5 minutes, until the roux relaxes. Slowly stir in the milk using a wire whisk. Raise the heat so that the sauce simmers gently for 5 minutes. Remove from the heat and set aside.

Preheat the oven to 350°F. Coat 10 to 12 shells with butter. In a medium-size mixing bowl, using a wire whisk, combine the egg, Worcestershire sauce, mustard, lemon juice, celery seed, hot pepper sauce, salt and pepper. Gently fold in the crabmeat. Pour the sauce over the crab mixture and fold to combine.

Place the shells on a baking sheet. Spoon the crab mixture into the shells and bake for 15 to 20 minutes, until the sauce is bubbly.

makes 10 to 12 shells

Pesto Rounds with Steak or Shrimp

These delicious bite-size appetizers pair the fresh garlicky taste of basil pesto with cooked shrimp or tender grilled flank steak. They're always a hit when I'm entertaining.

BASIL PESTO SAUCE

1   cup fresh basil

1   cup fresh parsley

4   garlic cloves

1   cup pine nuts or walnuts

¾   cup grated Parmesan cheese

¾   cup extra-virgin olive oil

PESTO ROUNDS

½   cup basil pesto sauce

2   tablespoons grated Parmesan cheese

1   French bread baguette, thinly sliced on a bias

1   pound shrimp, cooked, peeled

1   1-pound flank steak, grilled, thinly sliced

For sauce: Place the basil, parsley, garlic, nuts and Parmesan cheese in a food processor and process until the mixture forms a paste. Stop the machine and scrape down the sides. With the machine running, add the olive oil until all the oil is incorporated.

For pesto rounds: Combine the pesto and cheese. Spread on one side of each bread slice.

If making the shrimp rounds, top each slice with a shrimp and broil for 2 minutes until lightly toasted. Serve immediately.

If making the steak rounds, broil the bread and pesto mixture for 2 minutes, then top with the grilled flank steak. Serve warm or at room temperature.

makes 20 to 25 rounds

Crab and Salmon in Phyllo Cups

Everything except the crab and the purchased phyllo cups is blended in one bowl in this deceptively simple appetizer. It's one of my favorites. It takes no time to make, and the contrast of flaky phyllo and creamy seafood filling is always a hit with dinner guests.

2   2.1-ounce boxes frozen prebaked phyllo cups

4   ounces cream cheese, softened

½   cup shredded Cheddar cheese

1   3½-ounce can salmon, drained

¼   teaspoon dill

2   tablespoons mayonnaise

2   tablespoons buttermilk

1   teaspoon Worcestershire sauce

⅛   teaspoon lemon pepper seasoning

½   cup crabmeat, drained, picked over

Fresh dill for garnish

Thaw the prepared phyllo cups as directed on the box. Set aside.

In the mixing bowl of an electric mixer, combine the cream cheese, Cheddar cheese, salmon, $1/4$ teaspoon dill, mayonnaise, buttermilk, Worcestershire sauce and lemon pepper. Beat until well combined. Gently fold in the crabmeat.

Spoon the crab mixture into the phyllo cups and garnish with the fresh dill. Serve or chill for up to 2 hours.

makes 30 phyllo cups

Vegetable and Shrimp Tempura

— ● — ● — ● —

If you have farmer's markets in your neighborhood like we do, let their produce selection inspire you for this dish. The freshest summer vegetables will be perfectly complimented by the light, crispy tempura batter.

VEGETABLES AND SHRIMP

1	pound large shrimp
1	medium zucchini
1	red bell pepper
1	large onion
½	pound string beans
10	ounces mushrooms
1	gallon canola or corn oil for frying

BATTER

1⅔	cups all purpose flour
1½	cups corn starch
1	teaspoon salt
¼	cup chopped parsley
¼	cup sesame seeds
2	cups cold club soda

DIPPING SAUCE

½	cup fresh lemon juice
½	cup water
½	cup mirin
1	cup dark soy sauce
1	tablespoon sugar

For vegetables and shrimp: Peel the shrimp but leave on the tails. Devein and rinse well under cold water. Cut the zucchini ½-inch thick on a bias. Halve the red pepper. Remove the seeds, stem and inner fibers and then cut lengthwise into quarters. Peel and quarter the onion. Remove and separate the largest layers and discard the inside ones as they are too small to handle easily. Rinse and dry the green beans, leaving the ends intact. Wipe off any dirt that may cling to the mushrooms.

In a wide, deep pot, large enough to hold 4 inches of oil with 3 inches to spare to contain splatters, heat the oil to 360°F. Be sure to use a thermometer so that you can check that the oil remains as close to 360°F as possible throughout the cooking process.

For batter: In a medium-size mixing bowl, stir together the dry ingredients for the batter. Whisk in the club soda.

For dipping sauce: Whisk together all of the ingredients for the dipping sauce in a small mixing bowl and then transfer to individual ramekins for serving.

When the oil reaches 360°F be sure you have on hand a slotted spoon or a wire meshed strainer for removing the tempura and a baking sheet lined with paper towels for draining. Dip a piece of the cut vegetables into the batter and immediately place it in the oil. Do not allow the batter to run off the vegetable before placing in the oil. This may result in some messy counters, but disregard that until you are finished cooking.

Place just a few pieces of vegetables and shrimp in the oil at a time so that the temperature doesn't drop and they have enough room to float freely. The shrimp will take about 3 or 4 minutes to cook whereas the vegetables will be done in 1 or 2.

Remove the cooked tempura to the baking sheet lined with paper towels and place in a warm oven while you cook the remaining shrimp and vegetables, or serve immediately as they are best right out of the oil.

Serve the tempura on a large serving platter so that each person can choose what they like and dip in their own ramekin of sauce.

serves 6

Crab Quesadillas with Mango Salsa

When I served these at a neighborhood party, they disappeared long before any of the other party fare. You'll enjoy them with my signature salsa made with a surprising sweet and sour combination of mangos, ginger, red onion and seasonings.

SALSA

1   mango, peeled, pitted, diced

1   tablespoon lemon or lime juice

1   ½-inch piece ginger, peeled, grated

2   tablespoons chopped red onion

½   teaspoon hot pepper sauce (such as Tabasco)

3   or 4 cilantro sprigs, finely chopped

QUESADILLAS

¼   pound flaked crabmeat

1½   tablespoons chopped fresh cilantro

½   jalapeño pepper, seeded, minced

Safflower or vegetable oil

4   taco-size flour tortillas

2   cups shredded Monterey Jack cheese

For salsa: Mix together all of the ingredients for the salsa and chill.

For quesadillas: In a small bowl, mix together the crabmeat, cilantro and jalapeño.

Heat a 10-inch cast-iron skillet over medium heat and lightly coat with the oil. Place 1 tortilla in the pan, cook less than 1 minute and turn. Scatter 1 cup of the cheese on top of the tortilla. Top with an even layer of half the crab mixture and top with another tortilla. Press and cook until the cheese is melted and the tortillas are charred in spots, about 5 minutes total, turning frequently with a spatula. Transfer to a platter and repeat with the remaining ingredients. To serve, slice each quesadilla into quarters and top with the salsa.

serves 4

Crab Imperial Mushroom Caps

Mushroom caps filled with this rich crab mixture, then baked until lightly browned, are a divine appetizer for a special gathering. Try using some of the larger mushroom varieties if you're serving this as a main dish.

1 tablespoon unsalted butter

1 tablespoon all-purpose flour

1 cup half-and-half

1 tablespoon Sherry

Salt and freshly ground pepper to taste

1 teaspoon Chesapeake seasoning (such as Old Bay or JO)

1 pound crabmeat, drained, picked over

15 to 20 large mushroom caps

Preheat the oven to 350°F. In a medium-size saucepot over low heat, melt the butter. Add the flour and stir to combine the paste. Cook for 3 to 4 minutes, until the roux relaxes. Using a wire whisk, add the half-and-half in a slow stream. Whisk until smooth. Raise the heat to medium. When the sauce begins to bubble, add the Sherry, salt, pepper and Chesapeake seasoning. Gently fold in the crab and continue to cook until the mixture is just heated through.

Place the mushroom caps in a 8 x 11-inch baking dish. Spoon the crab mixture into the caps and bake for 15 to 20 minutes, until they are lightly browned on top.

makes 15 to 20 caps

MENU

Carrot Blini with Crabmeat and Caviar • 41

Lobster-Stuffed Tenderloin of Beef • 74

Sweet Potato and Pear Swirls • 113

Sautéed Snow Peas with Shallots • 110

Toasted Hazelnut Chocolate Marquise • 140

Carrot Blini with Crabmeat and Caviar

Few appetizers are as elegant or festive as this one inspired by the classic, centuries-old Russian dish. To some, the luxurious taste sensation of sour cream, crabmeat and caviar served on little buckwheat pancakes has no equal in culinary history.

1½ cups all-purpose flour

½ cup buckwheat flour

1 teaspoon salt

1½ cups milk

½ teaspoon active dry yeast

1 egg, separated

½ cup finely grated carrots

Butter

⅓ cup sour cream

½ cup crabmeat, drained, picked over

1 ounce osetra caviar

Sift the all-purpose and buckwheat flours with the salt into a small bowl. Scald the milk and allow to cool to room temperature. Sprinkle the yeast over the milk and whisk to incorporate. Add the egg yolk and whisk. Pour this mixture into the flour and stir until combined well. Set aside in a warm place and allow to rise for 2 hours. Beat with a wire whisk and let rise for another 1½ hours.

Just before serving, beat the egg white until it holds peaks and fold it into the batter. Gently fold in the grated carrots. Heat a heavy skillet over a medium flame and coat it lightly with butter. Pour a tablespoon of batter in the pan and allow it to spread before pouring the next pancake. Cook until the edges begin to bubble and then flip over to brown the other side. Remove to a plate and keep warm. Continue until batter is used up.

Place a scant teaspoon of sour cream on each blini. Top with a teaspoon of crabmeat. Place ¼ teaspoon of caviar in the center of the crabmeat and serve.

serves 8

Chorizo Puff Pastry

½   pound frozen puff pastry, thawed

¼   pound chorizo (Mexican sausage), cut in ¼-inch slices

1   egg yolk

Roll the puff pastry to a thickness of ⅛ inch. Cut it into circles ¼-inch larger than the chorizo slices. Center a slice of sausage on each circle; paint the edges of the dough with the egg and cover with another circle of puff pastry. Seal the edges well with a fork. Refrigerate each puff pastry as it is made so that the pastry does not soften too much. Place the puff pastries on a cookie sheet and bake at 450°F on the upper rack of the oven for 7 minutes or until lightly browned and puffed.

serves 6

California Deviled Crab Eggs

6   hard-boiled eggs

¾   cup crabmeat, drained, picked over

2   tablespoons chopped fresh chives

2   tablespoons mayonnaise

1   tablespoon rice vinegar

1   teaspoon wasabi paste

Salt and freshly ground pepper to taste

¼   small avocado

Sliced pickled ginger for garnish

Soy sauce for garnish

Cut the eggs in half. Remove the yolks and set the whites aside.

In a bowl, combine the yolks with the crab, chives, mayonnaise, rice vinegar and wasabi. Mix with a fork to blend. Season with the salt and pepper. Pile the yolk mixture into the whites, mounding high.

Cut the avocado into 12 equal pieces. Top each egg half with avocado. Arrange the eggs on a serving dish and serve with the ginger and soy sauce.

makes 12

Hot Spinach Dipping Sauce with Tortilla Chips

Hot jalapeño peppers add pizzazz and update this dip for its entertaining role. I like to make it in advance through all the steps until just before baking, when it can be refrigerated until later use.

2   4-inch hot green chili peppers, seeded, chopped

1   2-inch jalapeño pepper, minced, reserving some of the seeds

1   small onion, chopped

2   tablespoons vegetable oil

2   tomatoes, peeled, seeded, chopped

1   10-ounce package frozen chopped spinach, thawed, squeezed dry with towel

1   tablespoon red wine vinegar

1   8-ounce package cream cheese, room temperature

2   cups grated Monterey Jack cheese

1   cup half-and-half

Salt and freshly ground pepper to taste

Tortilla chips or crackers

In a small skillet, cook the pepper and onion in the oil over moderate heat, stirring, for 4 minutes or until the onion is softened. Add the tomatoes and cook the mixture, stirring, for 2 minutes. Transfer the mixture to a bowl and stir in the spinach, vinegar, cream cheese, Jack cheese, half-and-half and salt and pepper to taste. Transfer the dipping sauce to a buttered 10-inch round ovenproof serving dish and bake it in a preheated 400°F oven for 20 to 25 minutes or until it is hot and bubbly. Use tortilla chips or crackers for dipping.

serves 8

Phyllo Triangles with Crab

Biting into one of these flaky, spinach, crab and ricotta cheese appetizers is heavenly. They're one item my family insists on having at all our holiday gatherings. While they take a bit of time to prepare, they can be made ahead and frozen for impromptu parties.

½ pound fresh spinach or 1 10-ounce package frozen chopped, thawed, well drained

1 garlic clove

¼ teaspoon salt

½ medium onion

Vegetable spray

¾ pound ricotta cheese

⅛ teaspoon ground nutmeg or freshly grated

½ pound backfin crabmeat, drained, picked over

12 sheets frozen phyllo pastry sheets, thawed

2 tablespoons unsalted butter, melted

Destem, coarsely chop and briefly steam the spinach. Drain and cool. If using frozen, squeeze out the excess liquid and place in a medium mixing bowl. Chop the garlic with the salt until it becomes a paste.

Dice the onion. In a small, heavy skillet coated with vegetable spray, sauté the onion over medium heat until it becomes translucent and begins to give a sweet smell. In a medium bowl, combine the spinach, garlic, onion, ricotta and nutmeg. Gently fold in the crabmeat.

Preheat the oven to 450°F. Place a sheet of the phyllo on a lightly floured surface. Coat with vegetable spray. Lay a second sheet on top. Cut the phyllo into 5 strips crosswise. Place a heaping tablespoon of the crab mixture on the bottom edge of each strip. Fold from corner to corner, like folding a flag. Seal the ends with a brush of melted butter. Repeat the process with the remaining phyllo.

Place the triangles on an ungreased baking sheet and bake for 8 to 10 minutes until lightly browned.

makes 60 triangles

Fried Crab Wontons

I like the rhythm of filling and wrapping wontons, and then watching them turn golden brown in bubbling oil. Made with our handsome Chesapeake Bay crab, I think there are few foods more blissful to pop into your mouth.

DIPPING SAUCE

¼ cup orange marmalade

2 teaspoons vinegar

1 teaspoon hot pepper sauce (such as Tabasco) or hot mustard

WONTONS

½ pound flaked crabmeat

½ cup minced green onions

1 teaspoon garlic powder

Salt and freshly ground pepper to taste

About 20 wonton skins

Vegetable oil

For dipping sauce: Mix all of the ingredients together and set aside.

For wontons: In a bowl, combine the crab, green onions, garlic powder, salt and pepper.

Working on a counter with a cup of cold water nearby, top each wonton skin, one at a time, with a scant tablespoon of filling. Spread it in a line in the center and roll into a tight little cylinder. Seal the final edge by moistening the tip with water and pressing closed. Moisten, twist and seal the outside edges.

Fill a large skillet to a depth of 2 inches with oil and bring to 360°F, hot but not smoking. Fry the wontons a few at a time, turning once and cooking until golden all over, about 1 minute. Remove with a slotted spoon and drain on paper towels. Serve with the dipping sauce.

makes about 18 pieces

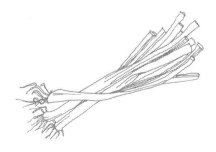

Baked Brie in Phyllo

I've been making this appetizer for years and my guests never fail to be delighted by the contrast of rich, creamy cheese and flaky pastry. Note that extra-ripe Brie will be very soft and may run from the rind when cut. Serve with baguette slices or crisp wheat crackers.

¼ cup apricot preserves (optional)

1 2-pound wheel Brie or Camembert cheese

½ pound frozen phyllo dough (10 to 12 18 x 14-inch sheets), thawed

½ cup unsalted butter or margarine, melted

Red and green grapes for garnish (optional)

Apples for garnish (optional)

Pears for garnish (optional)

Spread the preserves, if using, on top of the Brie. Wrap the Brie in the thawed phyllo dough, brushing each sheet with the melted butter. (Keep unused phyllo dough covered with a damp cloth while wrapping the Brie.) Turn the cheese over after applying a sheet of phyllo dough for even distribution. Brush the phyllo-wrapped Brie with the butter. Cover; refrigerate. Before serving, place the wrapped cheese in a shallow baking pan. Bake in a preheated 425°F oven for 8 to 12 minutes or till golden. Let stand for 10 minutes. Garnish with small bunches of grapes and slices of apples and pears, if desired.

serves 8 to 10

Baby Brie in Phyllo

Prepare Baked Brie in Phyllo as directed above except use 2 tablespoons apricot preserves, substitute 2 4 ½-ounce packages Brie or Camembert cheese for the 2-pound wheel, use ¼ pound phyllo dough (5 to 6 18 x 14-inch sheets), and ¼ cup melted butter or margarine. Continue as above, dividing the preserves, phyllo dough and butter between the cheese rounds.

Brie-Pecan Quesadillas

3 ounces Brie cheese, coarsely chopped (about ¼ cup)

2 8- to 9-inch flour tortillas

2 tablespoons toasted coarsely chopped pecans or walnuts

2 tablespoons snipped fresh Italian parsley

¼ cup sour cream

Parsley sprigs (optional)

Sprinkle the cheese over 1 tortilla. Top with the nuts and parsley. Top with the remaining tortilla, pressing gently.

Cook the quesadilla in a lightly greased 10-inch skillet over medium heat for 2 to 3 minutes or till lightly browned, turning once. To serve, cut each quesadilla into 8 wedges. Serve with sour cream and, if desired, garnish with the parsley sprigs.

serves 4

Brandied Blue Cheese, Walnut and Pear Crostini

6 ounces blue cheese, crumbled

3 tablespoons unsalted butter

2 tablespoons brandy

¼ cup coarsely chopped walnuts

16 ¼-inch-thick toasted French bread slices or baguette slices

1 medium ripe pear, cored, thinly sliced

Let the blue cheese and butter stand in a small bowl at room temperature about 30 minutes. Mash with a fork till well combined. Stir in the brandy and chopped walnuts. Top each slice of bread with a pear slice. Top each pear slice with 1 tablespoon of the blue cheese mixture.

Place the bread slices on a baking sheet. Broil 4 to 5 inches from the heat for about 2 minutes or till the cheese is melted and bubbly. Serve hot.

serves 8 to 12

MENU

Lime Marinated Crab and Shrimp • 49

Pasta with Smoked Salmon and Lemon Crème Fraîche • 101

Garlic Bread

Low-Fat White Chocolate Meringue Shells • 129

Lime Marinated Crab and Shrimp

Citrus, especially lemon, is always a perfect partner with seafood. In this recipe, lime flavors a tangy marinade for crab and shrimp—it's a refreshing twist that also enhances the tropical fruit garnish.

1½	teaspoons lime zest
½	cup lime juice
⅓	cup olive oil
3	tablespoons chopped fresh cilantro
1	jalapeño pepper, seeded, finely chopped
½	teaspoon freshly ground black pepper
2	garlic cloves, minced
1	tablespoon salt
1	pound shrimp, peeled, deveined
1	cup crabmeat, drained, picked over
2	heads endive
2	cups assorted fruit pieces (such as papaya chunks, kiwifruit, orange or lime sections)

In a medium mixing bowl, stir together the lime zest, lime juice, oil, cilantro, jalapeño, black pepper and garlic.

In a large saucepot, bring 1 quart of water and the salt to a boil. Add the shrimp and lower the heat to a simmer. Cook for 3 to 5 minutes, until the shrimp begin to turn opaque. Drain and place in a bowl of ice water until the shrimp are cooled.

Add the shrimp to the marinade and toss well. Cover and chill for 2 to 3 hours. During the last half hour, fold in the crabmeat.

Remove the leaves from the endive and place them on a platter or the individual plates. Drain the shrimp and crab. Place them in the center of the plate and surround with the pieces of fruit.

serves 10

Lobster-Filled Cream Puffs

These are definitely a luxury, but one so delectable I try to find excuses to make them. The nutty, sweet lobster salad enclosed in a bite-size cream puff is a heavenly morsel for any special occasion.

LOBSTER SALAD

1½ cups chopped cooked lobster meat

⅓ cup mayonnaise or salad dressing

1 to 2 tablespoons snipped fresh parsley, chives or tarragon

1 to 2 sweet red bell peppers, chopped

1 tablespoon lemon juice

Dash salt and freshly ground pepper to taste

CREAM PUFFS

1 cup water

6 tablespoons unsalted butter (no substitutes), cut up

1 teaspoon sugar

Dash salt

1 cup all-purpose flour

4 eggs

For lobster salad: Combine all of the ingredients together and set aside.

For cream puffs: Place the water, butter, sugar and a dash of salt in a heavy medium saucepan over medium heat till the butter melts and the mixture boils. Remove from the heat. Add the flour to the mixture all at once. Cook over low heat, stirring constantly with a wooden spoon, about 3 minutes or till the mixture is smooth and forms a ball that pulls away from the pan. Cool slightly (about 5 minutes). Place in a food processor bowl fitted with a metal cutting blade. Add the eggs one at a time and process till the mixture is thick and glossy.

Place the mixture in a pastry bag. Pipe 1-inch mounds about 1 inch apart onto an ungreased cookie sheet. Bake in a preheated 400°F oven for about 20 minutes till deep golden brown. Transfer to wire racks and cool.

To serve, cut the puffs open and fill each with a slightly rounded teaspoon of the lobster salad. If desired, cover the filled puffs and refrigerate up to 5 hours.

makes about 48

Crab Meat Mousse

This is one of those classic dishes that's been in my recipe box forever, but it never fails to perform when I need a showcase appetizer.

2 cups lump crabmeat, drained, picked over

1 tablespoon unflavored gelatin

¼ cup cold water

½ cup boiling water

½ cup mayonnaise

2 tablespoons finely snipped fresh chives or freeze-dried

2 tablespoons finely chopped fresh dill

1 tablespoon grated onion

1 tablespoon fresh lemon juice

Dash hot pepper sauce (such as Tabasco)

¼ teaspoon sweet paprika

1 teaspoon salt

¼ teaspoon Chesapeake seasoning (such as Old Bay or JO)

1 cup heavy cream

Dill sprigs for garnish

Clean the crabmeat and set aside in the refrigerator. Soften the gelatin in the cold water in a large mixing bowl for 3 minutes. Stir in the boiling water and slowly whisk until the gelatin dissolves. Cool to room temperature. Add the mayonnaise, chives, chopped dill, onion, lemon juice, a dash of hot pepper sauce, paprika, salt and Chesapeake seasoning and whisk until completely blended. Refrigerate until slightly thickened, about 20 minutes. Fold the crabmeat into the gelatin mixture. Whip the cream in a separate bowl until it forms soft peaks and fold gently into the crab mixture. Remove the mixture into a medium-size bowl or decorative 6- to 8-cup mold. Refrigerate, covered, at least 4 hours. Unmold the mousse onto a serving platter and garnish with the dill sprigs. Serve with black bread or crackers, or spoon into ripe avocado halves and serve as a first course.

serves 6

Crab Spring Roll

SALAD DRESSING

4   ounces orange marmalade

3   ounces white vinegar

⅛   teaspoon hot mustard

SPRING ROLLS

¼   head bok choy, coarsely shredded

4   green onions, cut into small pieces

2   slices Japanese pickled ginger, chopped

1   teaspoon chopped fresh cilantro

Salt and freshly ground pepper to taste

4   ounces crabmeat, drained, picked over

4   sheets spring roll wrappers

1   egg, beaten

Vegetable oil

4   cups mesclun salad or assorted leaf lettuce

1   grapefruit, peeled, sectioned, for garnish

For dressing: In a small bowl, whisk together the marmalade, vinegar and mustard. Set aside.

For spring rolls: Briefly blanch the bok choy in a pot of boiling, salted water. Drain using a skimmer or slotted spoon and place in a bowl. In the same pot of water, briefly blanch the green onions. Drain and dry with a paper towel. Add to the bowl of bok choy. Add the ginger, cilantro, salt and pepper and mix well. Gently fold in the crabmeat, taking care not to break up the lumps of crab.

Lay out the spring roll wrappers and brush the edges lightly with the beaten egg to help seal. Divide the crabmeat mixture among the wrappers, placing it in the center of the egg roll, and roll each one tightly.

Pour the oil into a deep, heavy frying pan to a depth of 1½ inches and heat until very hot, about 400°F. Deep-fry the rolls until golden brown. Remove and drain on paper towels. Cut each in half.

Place a bed of lettuce lightly dressed with the salad dressing on each of 4 plates. Top with 2 halves of a spring roll. Garnish the plate with the grapefruit.

serves 4

Cheese Torte

- - -

11 ounces goat cheese, crumbled

2 8-ounce packages Neufchâtel cheese

½ cup crumbled feta cheese

2 tablespoons prepared pesto

½ cup chopped golden raisins

⅓ cup chopped sun-dried tomatoes

⅓ cup pine nuts, toasted

Parsely sprigs for garnish

Line a springform pan with plastic wrap, letting the wrap extend over the sides. Using an electric mixer, blend the cheeses. Divide the mixture in half. Place half into the springform pan and spread evenly. Spread the pesto over the cheeses and sprinkle with half of the raisins, half of the tomatoes and half of the pine nuts. Spoon the remaining cheese over the top and spread until smooth. Sprinkle with remaining raisins and tomatoes. Cover the top with the overhanging plastic wrap and chill for 24 hours.

Remove the plastic wrap from the cheese and invert onto a serving platter. Surround with fresh parsley sprigs and pine nuts and serve with crackers or slices of French bread.

serves 12

Spinach Tortellini Soup

- - -

1½ tablespoons butter

2 garlic cloves, minced

1 small onion, sliced

6 cups chicken stock

1 10-ounce package frozen chopped spinach, thawed, drained

24 ounces cheese tortellini

Freshly grated Parmesan cheese

Over medium heat, sauté the butter, garlic and onion in a large stock pot. When the onion is translucent add the chicken broth and spinach. Bring to a boil and add the tortellini. Once the tortellini are tender, but not overcooked, serve with a sprinkle of Parmesan cheese on top.

serves 4 to 6

Maryland Crab Soup Supreme

This is my version of the classic soup, almost a stew, that's in the repertoire of every home cook in the state of Maryland. Specific ingredients and proportions vary, but the constants are crab, a beef bone or two, vegetables and, of course, Chesapeake seasoning.

1	pound stew meat, cubed
2	tablespoons corn oil
1	large onion, chopped
2	large celery stalks, chopped
1	large beef bone
12	whole crabs, cleaned
3	quarts water
½	teaspoon thyme
1	28-ounce can crushed tomatoes
¼	head cabbage, chopped
1	bay leaf
⅛	teaspoon cayenne pepper
Salt and freshly ground pepper to taste	
1	tablespoon Chesapeake seasoning
1	cup frozen corn kernels
1	cup string beans, cut into 1-inch pieces
1	cup frozen peas
3	large potatoes, peeled, diced
3	carrots, peeled, sliced
2	pounds lump crabmeat, drained, picked over

In a large, heavy kettle over high heat, sear the stew meat in the corn oil. After 3 minutes of searing, add the onion and celery. When the meat is browned, add the beef bone, whole crabs, water, thyme, tomatoes, cabbage, bay leaf, cayenne, salt, pepper and Chesapeake seasoning. Bring to a boil, then lower the heat and simmer for 1 to 1½ hours. Skim off any foam that floats to the surface.

Add the vegetables and cook until they are tender, about 5 minutes. If the soup is too thick, adjust with some water. Add the crabmeat and cook just until it is heated through. Serve immediately in large bowls.

serves 12

Cream of Crab Soup

Seafood soups are a staple in Chesapeake Bay kitchens, warming the heart and nourishing the soul. This rich, cream-based version of our region's classic crab soup is called a "bisque" and showcases the subtle flavors of the versatile blue crab.

8	tablespoons butter
1	cup flour
1½	teaspoons minced garlic
1½	teaspoons minced shallots
1	quart chicken stock
1	quart heavy cream
½	pound backfin crabmeat, drained, picked over
½	teaspoon Chesapeake seasoning (such as Old Bay or JO)
2	tablespoons chopped fresh parsley
1	tablespoon Sherry

In a 3-quart, heavy pot, melt the butter. Add the flour and stir until it becomes a paste. Cook over medium heat until the roux looks like wet sand. Add the garlic and shallots and cook for another 2 to 4 minutes.

While the roux is cooking, bring the chicken stock to a boil. When the roux is ready, using a wire whisk, gradually pour in the stock. Whisk until the roux is dissolved. Raise the heat and bring to a simmer for 15 minutes, stirring occasionally to avoid lumps. Add the cream and crab and heat through.

Just before serving, add the Chesapeake seasoning, parsley and Sherry.

serves 8

MENU

Crab and Salmon Chowder • 57

Asparagus and Crab Quiche • 70

Mesclun Salad

Palmiers • 133

Crab and Salmon Chowder

What's the difference between a chowder and a bisque? A chowder is a hearty soup, frequently made with chunks of seafood, while a bisque is a smooth, creamy soup. A favorite dish of seafarers, the word "chowder" was first used in North America in the 1730s.

3   slices bacon, chopped

2   medium leeks, thinly sliced

1   onion, thinly sliced

1   garlic clove, crushed

⅓   cup chopped fresh dill or 2 tablespoons dried

¾   teaspoon salt

½   teaspoon white pepper

3   cups fish stock or clam juice

1½ pounds small red potatoes, cut into 1-inch pieces

1   1-pound salmon fillet, cut into 1-inch pieces

1   cup crabmeat, drained, picked over

4   cups half-and-half

1   cup fresh or frozen corn kernels

In a large saucepot over medium heat, cook the bacon until crisp. Drain the fat, leaving 1 tablespoon in the pot. Add the leeks, onion and garlic and cook for 5 minutes until the leeks are soft. Stir in the dill, salt, white pepper, fish stock and potatoes.

Simmer gently, uncovered, for 15 to 20 minutes, until the potatoes are tender but not soft. Add the remaining ingredients and cook for 10 to 15 minutes, until the salmon is done.

serves 8

Lentil Stew

Slices of turkey sausage and a medley of chopped vegetables give this quick-cooking soup its bounty of nutrition and robust character. It's my family's favorite dish on cold, blustery nights when the wind tosses spray over the seawall in front of our house.

Vegetable spray

2   medium onions, chopped

4   garlic cloves, minced

8   ounces turkey sausage, sliced

½   teaspoon oregano

½   teaspoon freshly ground pepper

¼   teaspoon ground cumin

8   cups chicken stock

2   cups dried lentils

2   cups chopped stewed canned tomatoes (with juice)

2   tablespoons Worcestershire sauce

2   medium carrots, sliced

2   celery stalks, chopped

2   cups chopped spinach

Spray the bottom of a heavy, gallon-size pot with vegetable spray. Add the onions, garlic, turkey sausage and spices and sauté over medium heat until the sausage is browned.

Stir in the stock, lentils, tomatoes and Worcestershire sauce. Over high heat, bring the soup to a boil. Lower the heat and simmer for 15 minutes.

Add the vegetables, cover the pot and simmer for another 20 minutes.

serves 8 to 10

Crab Gazpacho

Always refreshing on a hot day, this cold Spanish vegetable soup takes on a sophisticated new personality when crabmeat is added. Served with a rustic loaf of bread and a black olive tapenade, it makes a perfect summer lunch or supper.

1	garlic clove
½	small onion, chopped
½	small green bell pepper, chopped
1	small cucumber, peeled, sliced
¼	teaspoon freshly ground pepper
3	ripe tomatoes, chopped
⅓	cup red wine vinegar
1	teaspoon salt
½	teaspoon chili powder
3	tablespoons olive oil
½	cup ice cubes
½	pound crabmeat, drained, picked over
½	cup croutons for garnish

Place all of the ingredients, except the crabmeat and croutons, in a food processor fitted with a metal blade. Pulse until smooth. Pour into 4 8-ounce soup bowls. Stir the crabmeat into each bowl and garnish with the croutons.

serves 4

MAINS

Crab Imperial with Smithfield Ham

Acclaimed as the king of Chesapeake Bay crab dishes, recipes for this richly spiced casserole are family heirlooms. This version of the famous dish gains its unique smoky flavor from another culinary legend, a slice of cured and aged Smithfield ham, Virginia's finest.

1	egg
⅔	cup mayonnaise
½	cup sour cream
2	tablespoons Dijon-style mustard
1	teaspoon Chesapeake seasoning (such as Old Bay or JO)
1	tablespoon chopped fresh parsley
1	pound crabmeat, drained, picked over
4	tablespoons unsalted butter, melted
1	sheet frozen puff pastry, thawed
8	paper-thin slices Smithfield ham
1	egg, beaten, for wash

Preheat the oven to 400°F. In a medium-size mixing bowl, beat the egg until fluffy. Add the mayonnaise, sour cream, mustard, Chesapeake seasoning and parsley and mix well. Gently fold in the crabmeat.

Brush the insides of 4 6-ounce ramekins with some of the melted butter. Using a ramekin as a template, cut out the puff pastry, leaving 1/4 inch to overlap the edges. Line each ramekin with 2 slices of ham. Spoon in the crab mixture. Top with the puff pastry and secure to the rim of each ramekin. Brush with the egg wash. Drizzle the top of each with the remaining melted butter.

Bake for 15 to 18 minutes or until golden brown. Serve at once.

serves 4

Chicken Kiev

These crisp, breadcrumb-coated packages of boneless chicken breast wrapped around fresh herbs transform the ordinary into extraordinary. First noted in Soviet Russia, the dish was probably a modern-day culinary creation for the first tourist hotels in that country.

1	teaspoon salt
½	teaspoon freshly ground pepper
6	skinless boneless chicken breasts, halved
6	garlic cloves, minced
2	teaspoons chopped fresh marjoram
2	teaspoons chopped fresh oregano
1	tablespoon lemon juice
1	tablespoon white wine
12	tablespoons (1½ sticks) unsalted butter, frozen
¼	cup flour
3	eggs, beaten
2	cups seasoned bread-crumbs or corn flakes

Sprinkle salt and pepper over both sides of the chicken breasts. In a small bowl, combine the garlic, marjoram, oregano, lemon juice and white wine. In the center of the underside of each chicken breast, place a tablespoon of butter and equal amounts of the herb mixture. Fold the 2 short ends towards the middle and then the 2 longer ends overlapping envelope-style to make a tight package.

Preheat the oven to 325°F. Dredge the chicken in the flour, then into the eggs and then the breadcrumbs. Place in a 9 x 13-inch baking dish and cook for 1 hour. Remove from the oven and serve.

serves 12

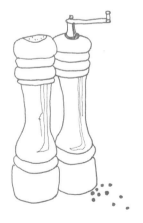

Crab Norfolk in Puff Pastry

Individual round puff pastries in this style are called "*vol-au-vent*" in France, meaning they "fly away in the wind" because of their lightness. Baked and immediately filled, this delicate dish must be served at once so the filling does not soak the tender pastry.

4	puff pastry shells
2	tablespoons unsalted butter
8	artichoke hearts, sliced
1	pound lump crabmeat, drained, picked over
8	ounces prosciutto ham, diced
2	ounces Sherry
2	cups heavy cream
Salt and freshly ground pepper to taste	
1	tablespoon chopped fresh parsley

Prepare the puff pastry according to the directions on the package.

In a medium-size, heavy skillet over medium heat, melt the butter. Add the artichokes, crab and prosciutto and sauté for 1 minute. Add the Sherry and cream and simmer until the liquid is reduced by half. Season with the salt and pepper.

Spoon the mixture into the pastry shells. Sprinkle with the parsley and serve immediately.

serves 4

Chicken Saltimbocca

This is a variation of the Italian dish made with veal that is a Roman specialty (but originally from Brescia). The name literally means "jump into the mouth," which I predict will easily occur after one taste of this succulent chicken adaptation.

3   boneless skinless chicken breasts, halved

6   slices boiled ham

3   slices mozzarella cheese, halved

1   medium tomato, diced

⅓   cup breadcrumbs

½   teaspoon sage

2   tablespoons chopped fresh parsley

2   tablespoons grated Parmesan cheese

4   tablespoons butter, melted

Place the chicken boned side up and cover with a piece of plastic wrap. Working from the center out, pound the chicken until it is a 5 x 5-inch shape. Remove the wrap. Repeat with the remaining chicken.

Place a slice of ham and half a slice of cheese on each chicken cutlet. Top with some tomato. Trim off any overlapping ham or cheese. Roll up jelly roll-style. Secure with a toothpick.

Preheat the oven to 350°F. In a wide, shallow bowl, combine the breadcrumbs, sage, parsley and Parmesan cheese. Place the melted butter in a shallow bowl. Dip each chicken roll in the butter and then roll in the crumb mixture. Place in a baking pan and cook for 40 minutes.

When the chicken has cooled slightly, remove the toothpicks. Cut each roll on a slight bias, ¹/₂-inch thick. Place in a curved, overlapping row on each plate.

serves 6

Braised Turkey Breast Cordon Bleu

The French phrase *"Cordon Bleu,"* originally indicated the blue ribbons worn by the highest order of medieval French knights. The term was extended to apply to food prepared at the highest culinary standards, perhaps because the aprons of French cooks were traditionally tied with blue ribbons.

2	tablespoons vegetable oil
2	tablespoons unsalted butter or margarine
1	whole bone-in 4-pound turkey breast
1	large onion, chopped
2	carrots, chopped
3	celery stalks, chopped
1	envelope or teaspoon instant chicken broth
½	teaspoon salt
½	teaspoon freshly ground pepper
¼	leaf thyme
½	cup water
5	tablespoons flour
1	cup light cream
¾	pound thinly sliced Canadian bacon
½	cup shredded Swiss cheese
	Watercress for garnish

Heat the oil and butter in a Dutch oven or flame-proof casserole dish. Add the turkey breast and brown evenly on all sides; remove the turkey.

Sauté the onion, carrots and celery in the Dutch oven until lightly browned. Stir in the chicken broth, salt, pepper, thyme and water. Heat to boiling; return the meat to the kettle; cover.

Braise in a slow oven (325°F) for 2 hours, basting often, or until the meat is tender (the juices run yellow when tender meat is pierced with a fork). Remove the meat to a carving board. Strain the cooking liquid into a 4-cup measuring cup, pressing the vegetables against the sieve to release as much juice as possible; discard the vegetables.

Skim off the fat. Return 4 tablespoons of the fat to the Dutch oven; stir in the flour; heat until bubbly; gradually add 2 cups of the cooking liquid (add water if there is not enough liquid) and the cream. Cook, stirring constantly, until the sauce thickens and bubbles—about 1 minute.

Carve the turkey meat in 1 piece from each side of the bone. Slice crosswise into 1/4-inch-thick slices. Arrange the slices alternating with the slices of Canadian bacon on the breast bone in a shallow baking dish. Stir the cheese into the sauce; pour over the meat. Refrigerate until ready to bake.

About 30 minutes before serving, place the dish in a moderate oven (350°F). Bake for 25 to 30 minutes or until heated through and the sauce is bubbling around the edges. If you wish, brown the top under the broiler. Garnish with the watercress.

serves 8

MENU

Lobster-Filled Cream Puffs • 50

Chicken Breasts with Crabmeat and Mozzarella • 67

Rice Pilaf

Green Beans

Easy Apple Tart • 127

Chicken Breasts with Crabmeat and Mozzarella

I like to dress up boneless chicken breasts by wrapping them around a stuffing of delicate crab and mild mozzarella cheese. Seasoned and sautéed until golden brown, they provide sophisticated flair to casual dinner parties.

½ cup tomato sauce

½ pound backfin crabmeat, drained, picked over

8 ounces mozzarella cheese, shredded

Salt and freshly ground pepper to taste

4 boneless skinless chicken breasts, halved, pounded thin

Kitchen string

4 tablespoons olive oil

Flour seasoned with salt and pepper

8 ounces mushrooms, quartered

3 tomatoes, peeled, deseeded, chopped

1 tablespoon chopped garlic

¾ cup dry Marsala

½ cup chopped fresh basil

1 teaspoon dried oregano

In a small mixing bowl, combine the tomato sauce, crabmeat and cheese. Season with the salt and pepper and toss well.

Flatten out each chicken breast. Spread 2 heaping tablespoons of the crab mixture on each breast, leaving an inch around the edges. Roll up and tie with 2 pieces of kitchen string. Pat dry with a paper towel and set aside.

In a large, heavy skillet over a medium flame, heat the oil. Lightly roll the chicken in the seasoned flour and place in the hot oil 1 breast at a time. Roll around so that it is browned all over. Remove from the pan and continue until all the chicken is browned.

Add the mushrooms to the skillet and sauté for 2 minutes. Add the tomatoes, garlic, Marsala, basil and oregano. Bring to a boil and return the chicken to the skillet. Cover, lower the heat to a gentle simmer and cook for 20 minutes. Turn the chicken twice during the cooking time.

Remove the chicken with a slotted spoon. Cut off the kitchen string. Bring the sauce to a boil and reduce until it is slightly thick. Pour the sauce over the chicken and serve.

serves 8

Grilled Chicken Sandwich with Roasted Red Onion and Garlic Mayonnaise

Use a round of focaccia bread to make this cosmopolitan sandwich. Grown-up taste buds will adore the garlicky mayonnaise spread and the melted cheese over the grilled chicken and spinach filling.

GARLIC MAYONNAISE

1	head garlic
3	½-inch slices red onion
2	tablespoons olive oil
¼	cup mayonnaise

SANDWICH

1	boneless skinless chicken breast
4	portobello mushrooms
½	cup olive oil for marinade
2	tablespoons olive oil
6	cups fresh spinach
1	loaf focaccia
¼	pound Gruyere cheese, grated

For garlic mayonnaise: Cut the top off the garlic to expose the cloves. Place on a baking sheet along with the onion slices. Drizzle with the olive oil and roast for 40 minutes. When browned remove from the oven and allow to cool slightly to make it easier to handle. Place in a food processor fitted with a metal chopping blade. Add the mayonnaise and process until smooth.

For sandwich: Preheat the oven to 375°F. Cut the chicken breast in half and the mushrooms into ¹/₂-inch slices. Marinate both in the ¹/₂ cup of olive oil for 10 minutes. In a large, heavy skillet over medium-high heat, or on a grill, cook the chicken and mushrooms for 10 to 15 minutes, turning frequently, until browned and cooked through. Remove from the heat and when slightly cooled cut the chicken into ¹/₂-inch slices.

In a large skillet over a high flame, heat the 2 tablespoons of olive oil. Add the spinach and toss to coat. Cover the skillet and cook for 3 to 5 minutes, until the spinach is just wilted. Remove from the skillet to a bowl.

Slice the focaccia horizontally to form a top and a bottom. Place under a broiler to toast the cut sides.

Put the bottom half of the focaccia on a baking sheet. Place the chicken slices like spokes of a wheel on the focaccia. Top with the spinach, then the mushrooms and then the cheese. Place under the broiler until the cheese melts.

Spread the top half of the focaccia with the garlic mayonnaise and place on top of the sandwich. Serve by cutting into 6 pie-shape wedges.

serves 6

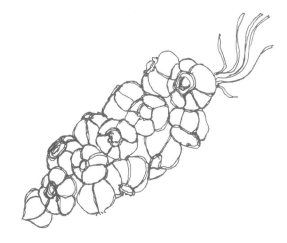

Asparagus and Crab Quiche

Pairing crab with asparagus is a natural, and my favorite way to celebrate spring. You could say this quiche is the Maryland variation of the classic cheese and egg tart.

1	9-inch deep-dish pie shell
1	pound fresh asparagus
4	slices bacon, cooked, drained, crumbled
4	ounces Swiss cheese, grated
4	ounces Cheddar cheese, grated
½	cup crabmeat, drained, picked over
4	eggs
1½	cups half-and-half
⅛	teaspoon ground nutmeg or freshly grated
½	teaspoon salt
¼	teaspoon freshly ground pepper

Preheat the oven to 400°F. Bake the pie shell for 10 minutes. Remove from the oven and then reduce the heat to 375°F.

Bring a saucepot of salted water to a boil. Cut the asparagus into ½-inch pieces and add to the boiling water. Cook for 3 to 5 minutes. Drain and run under cold water until cool.

Sprinkle the bacon crumbs into the pie shell with the cheese, asparagus and crab. Beat the eggs, half-and-half, nutmeg, salt and pepper and pour into the pie shell. Bake for 40 minutes.

serves 8

Beef Tenderloin

I like to use my special rub of herbs, olive oil, chipotle peppers and garlic when preparing this choice cut of beef. It adds a subtle complexity of flavor that enhances the meat's rich taste.

1 tablespoon finely chopped seeded dried chipotle peppers

1 tablespoon chopped fresh oregano or 1 teaspoon crushed dried

1 tablespoon olive oil

1 teaspoon cumin

½ teaspoon salt

2 garlic cloves, crushed

2 pounds beef tenderloin

For the rub, combine the chipotle peppers, oregano, oil, cumin, salt and garlic. Spread over the surface of the meat, rubbing in with your fingers. Cover and refrigerate for 6 to 24 hours.

Preheat the oven to 350°F. Place the meat on a rack in a shallow roasting pan. Insert a meat thermometer into the center of the roast. Roast for 45 minutes. At this time test the meat with the meat thermometer for doneness (120°F for rare, 140°F for medium and 150°F for well-done). Let the meat rest for 15 minutes before slicing.

serves 4 to 6

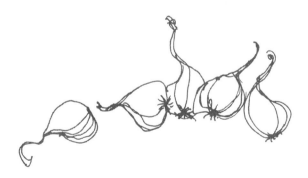

MENU

Steamed Crabs Maryland Style • 73

Grilled Corn on the Cob with Chili Butter • 111

Bacon Potato Salad • 119

Tomato and Basil Vinaigrette

Crunchy Coleslaw • 117

Blueberry Shortcakes • 130

Steamed Crabs Maryland Style

Northerners may boil their lobsters, but here in the Chesapeake Bay region we'd never dream of such a thing. We simply steam our big blue jimmies in pots on top of the stove. It's another local culinary ritual that's more a process than a recipe, but every family has their own way of doing it. You do what you saw your mother doing and don't ask why.

2	cups water
1	cup beer
1	cup cider vinegar
1	dozen live hard-shell crabs
4	tablespoons Chesapeake seasoning (such as Old Bay or JO)
3	tablespoons rock salt
½	cup unsalted butter, melted
1	lemon, cut into eighths
¼	cup Chesapeake seasoning (such as Old Bay or JO)
	Hot pepper sauce (such as Tabasco)

In a large pot with a rack raised 2 inches from the bottom, place the water, beer and vinegar. Place 1 layer of the crabs on the rack and sprinkle with some Chesapeake seasoning and rock salt. Continue to layer and season the crabs until they are all in the pot. Bring the liquid to a boil, cover the pot and steam the crabs for 20 minutes.

When the crabs are cooked, remove them to a platter. Provide knives, mallets and shell crackers. Serve with pots of melted butter, wedges of lemons, an extra dish of Chesapeake seasoning and a bottle of hot pepper sauce.

serves 6

Lobster-Stuffed Tenderloin of Beef

Pure indulgence, of course! But I love to treat my husband Ron with one of his favorite meals after we've been working especially hard. After all these years, the way to a man's heart is still through his stomach.

2   4-ounce frozen lobster tails

1   3- to 4-pound beef tenderloin

1   tablespoon unsalted butter, melted

2   teaspoons lemon juice

Cotton string

6   slices bacon

½   cup sliced green onions

½   cup unsalted butter

½   cup dry white wine

⅛   teaspoon garlic salt

Preheat the oven to 425°F. Bring a medium-size pot with a few inches of salted water to a boil. Add the lobster tails. Return to a boil. Reduce the heat and simmer for 5 minutes. While the lobster is cooking, cut the tenderloin lengthwise to within ½ inch of the bottom to butterfly. Remove the lobster tails from the water and when cool enough to handle, remove them from their shells and slice in half lengthwise. Place the lobster, end to end, inside the beef.

In a small cup, combine the melted butter and the lemon juice. Drizzle it over the lobster. Close the meat over the lobster and tie shut at intervals of 1 inch with cotton string.

Place the meat on a rack in a roasting pan. Cook for 45 to 50 minutes for rare meat (120°F internal temperature). Approximately 20 minutes into the roasting, place the bacon strips over the meat.

In a small, heavy saucepot over very low heat, cook the green onions in the butter. Add the wine and garlic salt and heat through, stirring frequently.

When the roast is done, remove from the oven and allow it to rest for 15 minutes before cutting. Slice into 1-inch slices and spoon some of the wine sauce over each piece.

serves 8

London Broil

This is another of Ron's favorites when he's not eating some form of crab. My tip for broiling this classic steak: the hotter the better. If it's cooked medium or well-done, it will become extremely tough.

1   2-pound flank steak

1   tablespoon vegetable oil

2   teaspoons chopped fresh parsley

1   garlic clove, crushed

1   teaspoon salt

1   teaspoon lemon juice

⅛   teaspoon freshly ground pepper

1   medium onion

1   tablespoons olive oil

1   tablespoon red wine

Wipe the steak with damp paper towels and trim the fat from the steak.

In a cup, combine the oil, parsley, garlic, salt, lemon juice and pepper. Brush half of the oil mixture over the top of the steak.

Place the steak, oiled side up, on a lightly greased broiler pan. Broil, 4 inches from the heat, for 5 minutes. Turn the steak; brush with the remaining oil mixture and broil 4 to 5 minutes longer—at this point the steak will be rare, which is the only way London broil should be served.

In a medium size, heavy skillet over low heat, slowly sauté the onions in the oil. When they become translucent and slightly browned, add the red wine. Simmer for one minute more and remove from the skillet..

Slice the steak very thinly, on the diagonal and across the grain. Serve with the onions.

serves 4

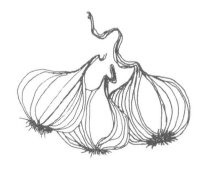

Spare Ribs with Sauerkraut and Apples

Being practical folk, we love to make one-pot meals in the Chesapeake Bay region. This hearty dish acknowledges our German forebears and highlights the natural attraction between savory sauerkraut, tart apples and caraway seeds.

6	tablespoons unsalted butter
4	slices bacon, cut into 1-inch pieces
1	small onion, thinly sliced
1	tart apple (such as Stayman or Pippin), peeled, cored, thinly sliced
2	pounds sauerkraut, drained, lightly rinsed
Salt and freshly ground pepper to taste	
½	teaspoon caraway seeds
4	pounds spare ribs

Preheat the oven to 350°F. In a large, heavy saucepot over medium heat, melt the butter and render the bacon for a few minutes. Add the onion and apple and sauté for 3 to 4 minutes. Add the sauerkraut to the pot. Add the salt, pepper and caraway seeds. Toss well and bring to a boil. Lay the ribs on top, cover tightly and place in the oven for 1 hour.

Remove from the oven, cut the ribs into individual ribs and serve.

serves 8

Southwestern Pot Roast

A medley of dried chilies in the cooking sauce and a rub of exotic spices like cumin and coriander add pizzazz to this pot roast. Keep the mystery ingredient—chocolate chips blended into the rich serving sauce—a secret and make everyone guess your surprise.

3	tablespoons chili powder
1	tablespoon ground cinnamon
1	tablespoon salt
1	teaspoon cumin
½	teaspoon coriander
4	tablespoons olive oil
3	pounds bottom round of beef
2	cups chopped onions
5	dried chilies (combination of New Mexico, Ancho and Pasilla)
10	whole garlic cloves
½	cup chicken stock
2	cups chopped tomatoes
1	tablespoon molasses
1	teaspoon dried oregano
3	6-inch tortillas, cut into strips
1	tablespoon semisweet chocolate chips
¼	to 1 cup chicken stock

Combine the chili powder, cinnamon, salt, cumin, coriander and 3 tablespoons of the olive oil and rub onto the meat. In a large, heavy skillet over low heat, sauté the onions, chilies and garlic in the remaining tablespoon of olive oil for 5 to 7 minutes, until the onions are translucent. Deglaze the pan with the ½ cup of chicken stock. Add the tomatoes, molasses, oregano and tortilla strips. Bring to a simmer.

Preheat the oven to 350°F. Place the meat in a large, heavy, ovenproof pot. Add the tomato mixture. Bring to a simmer, cover and place in the oven. Roast for 3 hours, until the meat is very tender. Remove the meat to a cutting board and pour the sauce into a blender. Add the chocolate chips and enough chicken stock to make the sauce thin enough to pour, while the machine is running.

Cut the meat into 1-inch slices and cover with the sauce.

serves 6

MENU

Spinach Tortellini Soup • 53

Crabmeat Omelet • 79

Braised Leeks

Crème Caramel • 139

Crabmeat Omelet

●　　●　　●

A basic dish since the Middle Ages, a simple omelet takes on aristocratic style with a crabmeat and mushroom filling. Some cooks recommend beating the yolks and whites separately to create a fluffier omelet, but I take the simple, one-bowl path in my kitchen.

3	tablespoons unsalted butter
1	teaspoon minced shallot
¼	cup sliced mushrooms
1	tablespoon dry Sherry
¼	pound crabmeat, drained, picked over
4	eggs, room temperature
½	teaspoon salt
½	teaspoon freshly ground pepper
1	tablespoon chopped fresh parsley
2	tablespoons butter

In a small, heavy skillet over low heat, melt 1 tablespoon butter. Add the shallot and sauté for 2 minutes. Add the mushrooms and cook until they soften. Raise the heat, add the Sherry and deglaze the pan by scraping any bits on the bottom.

Place the crabmeat in a medium mixing bowl. Add the mushroom mixture and combine gently.

Melt 1 tablespoon of butter over medium heat in an 8-inch omelet pan. In a small mixing bowl, using a wire whisk, beat 2 of the eggs with half of the salt and pepper until frothy. Beat in half of the parsley. Pour the eggs into the pan and swirl around to coat the pan with egg. When the edges begin to turn opaque, place half of the crab mixture across the center, bisecting the omelet. When most of the omelet has become opaque, loosen the edges with a spatula and fold the sides over the filling. Tip the pan along the side of the serving plate and roll the omelet onto it.
Repeat the omelet making process for the second omelet. Serve immediately.

serves 2

Crab Crepes

In France where they originated, crepes were served on Candlemas and Shrove Tuesday as a symbol of renewal and hopes for future happiness and good fortune. Now popular around the world, these thin pancakes are delightful filled with crab in a classic white sauce.

CREPE BATTER

1	cup all-purpose flour
¼	teaspoon salt
1	egg
1	egg yolk
1¼	cups milk
2	tablespoons unsalted butter, melted

VELOUTE SAUCE

3	tablespoons unsalted butter
3	tablespoons flour
1½	cups chicken or fish stock
½	cup milk
¼	cup dry white wine
Pinch	salt and freshly ground pepper

For crepe batter: In a medium-size mixing bowl, combine the flour and salt. Make a well in the center and add the egg, egg yolk, milk and 1 tablespoon of the melted butter. Beat well and set aside to rest for 2 hours.

Brush the bottom and sides of a small skillet or crepe pan with the remaining tablespoon of butter. Over medium-high heat, add 2 tablespoons of the batter to the pan and swirl to coat the bottom and slightly up the sides of the pan. Cook for 1 or 2 minutes, until the top looks dry. Loosen the edges with a metal spatula and flip the crepe over to cook for another 30 seconds. Place the crepes between layers of waxed paper and set aside. This will make about 12 to 15 crepes. Choose the best 4 and refrigerate the rest for another use.

For Veloute sauce: In a small saucepot over medium heat, melt the butter. Add the flour and stir until a paste is formed. Lower the heat and cook the roux until it begins to relax, about 5 minutes. While the roux is cooking, in another small pot bring the stock to a boil. Stirring with a wire whisk, gradually add the stock to the roux. Stir vigorously until the sauce is smooth. Raise the heat to medium and bring the sauce to a boil. Add the milk. Lower the heat to a simmer and cook

CREPES FARCIES ET ROULEU (CRAB-STUFFED FRENCH PANCAKES)

1 tablespoon unsalted butter

2 tablespoons sliced green onions

¼ cup chopped mushrooms

½ pound lump crabmeat, drained, picked over

2 cups Veloute sauce

¼ cup grated Swiss cheese

for 5 minutes. Add the wine and the salt and pepper. Remove the pot from the heat.

For crepes: Preheat the oven to 400°F. In a medium-size saucepot, melt the butter over medium heat. Add the green onions and mushrooms and sauté for 2 to 3 minutes. Add the crabmeat and 3/4 cup of the Veloute sauce.

Place a crepe in a buttered 8 x 11-inch baking dish. Spoon 1/4 of the crab mixture across the center of the crepe and fold the side over the top. Place the stuffed crepe at the end of the baking dish and repeat the process with 3 more crepes.

Pour the remaining Veloute sauce over the crepes and sprinkle with the Swiss cheese. Bake for 20 minutes or until the sauce is bubbling.

serves 4

Salmon in Puff Pastry with Thyme Butter

Every waterman worth his salt loves this richly flavored red or pink fish, and I love serving them this dramatic dish. The combination of a crisp puff pastry crust wrapped around the poached fillet with its cream cheese and mushroom topping is simply divine.

SALMON

1	cup dry white wine or chicken broth
1	cup water
2	pounds salmon fillet, skinned
1	tablespoon unsalted butter
4	green onions, chopped
¾	pound mushrooms, sliced
4	ounces cream cheese, softened
1	17-ounce box frozen phyllo puff pastry, thawed
1	egg, beaten, for wash

THYME BUTTER

½	cup unsalted butter
2	teaspoons dried thyme
1	tablespoon lemon juice

For salmon: In a large skillet, bring the wine and water to a simmer. Add the salmon, cover and poach for 8 to 10 minutes, until the salmon is opaque and slightly flaky. At this point the salmon can be removed from the poaching liquid, covered in plastic wrap and chilled a day ahead.

In a medium-size, heavy skillet over medium heat, melt the butter. Add the green onions and sauté for 2 minutes. Add the mushrooms and cook for 5 to 8 minutes, until most of the mushroom liquid has evaporated. Stir in the cream cheese until well blended. Remove from the heat.

Preheat the oven to 400°F. Roll 1 sheet of puff pastry on a lightly floured surface into a 14 x 10-inch rectangle. Place half of the salmon in the center of the pastry, leaving a 3-inch border all around. Spread half of the mushroom mixture on the top. Brush the pastry border with some egg wash and fold it over the top of the prepared fish. Pinch the pastry to secure the edges. Place carefully, seam-side down, on a buttered baking sheet. Repeat the procedure with the remaining fish and mushroom mixture. Brush the tops of the pastry with any remaining egg wash.

Bake for 25 to 35 minutes or until the puff pastry is golden brown. Remove from the oven and allow to stand for 10 minutes.

For thyme butter: Place all of the ingredients in a small, heavy saucepot over medium heat. Cook and stir until well blended. Slice the salmon and pour a couple of tablespoons of thyme butter over each serving of salmon.

serves 8 to 10

Crab, Cheese and Bacon Frittata

6   eggs

1   cup milk

1   green onion, finely chopped

2   tablespoons unsalted butter, melted

½   teaspoon salt

⅛   teaspoon freshly ground pepper

4   ounces Cheddar cheese, shredded

4   slices bacon, cooked, drained, crumbled

¾   cup crabmeat, drained, picked over

Preheat the oven to 400°F. Coat the bottom and sides of a 9-inch pie pan with butter.

In a medium mixing bowl, using a wire whisk, beat together the eggs, milk, green onion, butter, salt and pepper. Gently fold in the cheese, bacon and crabmeat. Bake for 20 to 30 minutes or until the eggs are set and beginning to brown.

serves 8

MENU

Romaine Salad with Balsamic Vinaigrette

Crabmeat au Gratin • 85

High-Rise Apple Pancake • 142

Crabmeat au Gratin

A melted cheese topping and a delicate Sherry-flavored cream sauce make this dish a perfect showcase for crab. Serve over buttered toast or steamed rice with a green salad for a light lunch or supper.

6 tablespoons unsalted butter

1 cup thinly sliced green onions

2 tablespoons chopped fresh parsley

3 tablespoons flour

Salt and freshly ground pepper to taste

1½ cups milk

1 tablespoon dry Sherry

2 pounds crabmeat, drained, picked over

1 cup shredded Cheddar cheese

Preheat the oven to 350°F. In a medium skillet over low heat, melt the butter and sauté the green onions and parsley until they are tender, 2 to 4 minutes. Add the flour and stir until combined. Season with salt and pepper. Using a wire whisk, gradually add the milk. Whisk until smooth. Simmer for 5 minutes. Remove from the heat and stir in the Sherry.

Place the crabmeat in a large, ovenproof casserole and pour the milk mixture over it. Fold gently to combine. Sprinkle with the cheese and bake for 20 minutes, until the cheese has melted and the sauce is bubbling.

serves 8

Crab with Smithfield Ham

½   pound Smithfield ham, diced

3   tablespoons butter

1   pound crabmeat, drained, picked over

½   cup dry white wine

2   cups cooked rice

In a large, heavy skillet over medium heat, sauté the ham in the butter for 5 to 6 minutes. Add the crabmeat and stir gently to heat through. Add the wine. Spoon the crab mixture over the rice and serve.

serves 4

Puff Pastry with Crab

2   puff pastry shells

2   tablespoons unsalted butter

2   green onions, sliced

½   teaspoon chopped fresh dill

2   tablespoons flour

½   cup milk

1   tablespoon lemon juice

Salt and freshly ground pepper to taste

¼   cup heavy cream

½   pound crabmeat, drained, picked over

Bake the puff pastry shells according to the directions on the package. In a large, heavy skillet over low heat, melt the butter. Add the green onions and dill and cook for 2 minutes. Stir in the flour and sauté for 3 minutes more. Using a wire whisk, add the milk and stir quickly to avoid lumps. Simmer for 2 to 4 minutes, until thick and smooth. Stir in the lemon juice and salt and pepper. Add the cream and cook for another 2 minutes. Add the crab and fold in gently to combine.

Spoon the crab mixture into the shells and serve immediately.

serves 2

Baked Stuffed Rockfish

The most popular finfish taken from Chesapeake waters, rockfish is actually a striped bass. Once overfished, the species is now successfully recovering through fish farms and careful conservation. A white fish with a flaky, slightly oily flesh, it's delicious baked whole or stuffed.

1   pound backfin crabmeat, drained, picked over

6   tablespoons unsalted butter, melted, cooled

Juice of 1 lemon

Salt and freshly ground pepper to taste

2   tablespoons chopped fresh parsley

1   3- to 3½-pound whole rockfish, boned

Milk as needed

4   strips hickory smoked bacon

Preheat the oven to 350°F. Place the crabmeat in a bowl, pour the melted butter and lemon juice over the top and toss. Season with salt and pepper. Mix in the parsley. Stuff the crab mixture inside the fish and secure with skewers or toothpicks. Cover the bottom of a baking dish large enough to hold the fish comfortably with milk, about ¼ inch deep. Place the fish in the dish. Sprinkle lightly with salt and pepper. Top with the bacon.

Bake for 40 to 45 minutes or until the fish flakes at the touch of a fork. Baste occasionally during the baking with the milk from the dish. When done, transfer the fish to a serving platter. Remove the bacon and discard. Remove the toothpicks. Pour any remaining cooking liquid over the fish and serve.

serves 4

Grilled Tuna with Eggplant Tapenade

Always look for a deep red color to ensure the freshness of tuna. Whether you prepare the tuna on a gas grill or on the stovetop, the taste and texture of this meaty fish find a perfect complement in the earthy flavors of an eggplant and Kalamata olive tapenade.

TAPENADE

1   large eggplant

¼   cup plus 1 teaspoon olive oil

4   garlic cloves, roasted or minced

1   cup pitted Kalamata olives

2   teaspoons capers, rinsed

1   teaspoon coarsely ground pepper

2   anchovy fillets

TUNA

1½   pounds tuna

1   tablespoon olive oil

Salt and freshly ground pepper to taste

For tapenade: Preheat the oven to 425°F. Coat the eggplant with the 1 teaspoon olive oil. Place the eggplant on a baking sheet and roast it for about 20 minutes or until the skin is blistered and brown. Set aside and peel when cool enough to handle. Place the eggplant, garlic, olives, capers, pepper and anchovies in a food processor and blend. Once the mixture is pureed, drizzle in the remaining olive oil. Process until the mixture looks like a rough paste.

For tuna: Brush both sides of the tuna with the olive oil and then salt and pepper. Grill for about 4 to 5 minutes per side. Do not overcook the tuna or it will be dry. Tuna can also be done in a pan with very hot oil; sear it on both sides for 4 to 5 minutes per side.

Serve the tapenade at room temperature with the tuna.

serves 2

Tuna with Sautéed Spinach and Béarnaise Sauce

BÉARNAISE SAUCE

2	tablespoons red wine vinegar
2	teaspoons chopped green onion
½	teaspoon tarragon
⅛	teaspoon freshly ground pepper
4	egg yolks
¾	cup unsalted butter, softened
1	tablespoon chopped fresh parsley

SPINACH

1	pound fresh spinach, washed well, stems removed
3	tablespoons unsalted butter
2	shallots, minced
2	garlic cloves, minced

TUNA

2	small tuna steaks (1½ pounds total)
1	tablespoon olive oil

For béarnaise sauce: In the top of a double boiler, combine the first 4 ingredients. Over high heat, heat to boiling and boil until the vinegar is reduced to about 1 tablespoon. Place the top of the double boiler over the bottom of the double boiler containing hot, not boiling, water. Add the egg yolks and cook, beating constantly with a wire whisk until slightly thickened. Add the butter, about 2 tablespoons at a time, beating constantly with the whisk, until the butter is melted and the mixture is thickened. Stir in the parsley. Set aside.

For spinach: Chop the spinach coarsely and set aside. In a large sauté pan over medium heat, melt the butter. Add the shallots and garlic. Sauté until they begin to give off their aroma, about 2 to 3 minutes. Add the spinach and sauté until it wilts.

For tuna: Turn the oven to broil and set the oven rack 4 to 5 inches below the flame. Brush both sides of the tuna steaks with the olive oil. Place them on a broiling pan and broil for 5 minutes. Turn and cook for another 3 to 5 minutes. Check for doneness. Remember that the fish will continue to cook after it is removed from the oven. The fish should have some pink in the center.

To serve, put some of the spinach on a plate and top with sautéed or grilled tuna. Top with the béarnaise sauce.

serves 2

M E N U

Pesto Rounds with Shrimp • 34

Fried Soft-Shell Crabs in Beer Batter • 91

Oven Baked French Fries

Grilled Corn on the Cob with Chili Butter • 111

Peaches and Cream Casserole • 126

Fried Soft-Shell Crabs in Beer Batter

The blue crab's amazing summer molting process, a natural part of its growth cycle in the shallow waters of the Chesapeake Bay, gives us with this culinary delicacy. This preparation is authentic, simple and remarkably delicious.

5   cups all-purpose flour

½   cup cornstarch

1   tablespoon salt

1   teaspoon white pepper

1   tablespoon garlic powder

1   tablespoon onion powder

1   cup beer (not light)

Canola oil

12   soft-shell crabs, cleaned

Sift together the dry ingredients. Stir into the beer and let stand at room temperature for 1 hour.

In a medium-size, heavy skillet bring about 3 inches of canola oil to 350°F over a high flame. Dip the crabs, 2 at a time, in the batter and then place into the oil. Cook for about 2 minutes and then turn them over and cook for another minute. Remove to a baking sheet lined with a paper towels. Keep warm in a closed oven while you fry the remaining crabs.

serves 6

Steamed Mussels and Roasted Garlic Sabayon

This dish illustrates the simple, straightforward style that is a hallmark of Chesapeake cookery. Mussel lovers will discover that the rich garlic-infused sabayon sauce elevates these shellfish close to a unique culinary experience.

2	pounds mussels
1½	pounds small new red potatoes or any new potatoes
1	tablespoon white vinegar
1½	cups white wine or more if needed
4	3-inch rosemary sprigs
4	egg yolks
1½	tablespoons roasted garlic paste*
1½	teaspoons salt
½	teaspoon freshly ground pepper

Juice of 1 lemon

Rosemary sprigs and blossoms (if available) for garnish

Scrub and de-beard the mussels. Wash the potatoes and cut them in half, if they are larger than a walnut. Fill a large pot with cool, salted water and add the potatoes and vinegar. Bring to a boil over high heat, then reduce the heat to a low boil and continue to cook until tender, about 10 minutes. Drain and keep the potatoes warm. Put the mussels, wine and rosemary in a large pan and cover tightly. Set the pan over high heat and steam just until the mussels open, about 3 to 4 minutes. Transfer the mussels to a large bowl and cover to keep warm; discard any mussels that do not open.

Pour the mussel nectar from the pan through a fine sieve; discard the rosemary sprigs. Also strain any mussel nectar that has collected in the bottom of the bowl. Measure 1½ cups of the nectar, adding white wine if there is not enough nectar. Combine the egg yolks, roasted garlic paste, salt and pepper in a medium, stainless steel bowl and whisk until smooth. Add the measured mussel nectar and the lemon juice. Set the bowl on top of a saucepan of boiling water (the water should not touch the bottom of the bowl). Whisk vigorously until the sabayon is frothy and thickened and there is no trace of liquid at the bottom of the bowl, about 3 to 5 minutes. Place the potatoes alongside the mussels and pour the sabayon over the mussels. Garnish with the sprigs and blossoms of rosemary.

* To make garlic paste: Bake whole heads of garlic (wrapped in foil) at 400°F for 45 minutes. Let cool slightly, then separate the cloves. Squeeze out the tender garlic and mash with a fork in a small bowl. (One large head of garlic should yield the 1 1/2 tablespoons needed here.)

serves 4

Sautéed Soft-Shell Crabs with Lemon Basil Butter Sauce

Centered in Crisfield, Maryland, the Chesapeake Bay supplies 90 percent of the U.S. soft-shell crab industry. Shipped fresh or frozen to the finest restaurants around the world, soft-shell crabs are perfect prepared in this straightforward, traditional style.

2   cups all-purpose flour

1   tablespoon Chesapeake seasoning (such as Old Bay or JO)

½   teaspoon salt

¼   teaspoon freshly ground pepper

6   tablespoons unsalted butter for sautéing

12   soft-shell crabs, cleaned

8   tablespoons unsalted butter

Juice of 1 lemon

¼   cup chopped fresh basil

In a shallow bowl, stir together the flour, Chesapeake seasoning, salt and pepper. In a large, heavy skillet, melt half of the butter. Dredge the crabs in the flour mixture and place, 2 at a time, in the skillet. Sauté the crab until they are light brown and crisp, about 4 minutes. Turn them over and brown on the other side, about 3 to 4 minutes. Add the remaining butter as needed while sautéing the rest of the crabs. Remove to a baking sheet lined with a paper towels and keep warm in a closed oven.

In a small, heavy saucepot, melt the 8 tablespoons of butter. Add the lemon juice and basil and heat through. Ladle a couple of tablespoons over each crab serving.

serves 6

Sesame Shrimp and Asparagus

I call this my spring time stir-fry. When the days grow longer and the first tender asparagus spears show up in the market, this dish always assures me that spring is truly just around the corner.

2	small onions
1½	pounds asparagus
1	tablespoon sesame seeds
2	tablespoons corn oil
1½	pounds shrimp, peeled, deveined
1	tablespoon plus 1 teaspoon soy sauce
1	lemon, quartered, for garnish

Halve and thinly slice the onions across the grain. Clean and cut the asparagus into 2-inch lengths. In a large skillet over medium heat, toast the sesame seeds until golden. Remove to a small bowl as soon as they start to turn brown.

Bring a small pot of water to a boil and blanch the asparagus for 3 to 5 minutes, until tender. Drain and set aside.

Add the corn oil to the skillet, raise the heat to medium-high and sauté the asparagus, onions and shrimp. Stir frequently and cook until the shrimp are opaque and pink and the asparagus is tender. Stir in the sesame seeds and soy sauce. Garnish with lemon and serve immediately over rice or noodles.

serves 4

Crab Swiss Quiche

I make this versatile dish for lunch or a simple Sunday night supper. The creamy egg custard and the nutty flavor of Swiss cheese are perfect flavor accents for crab.

1	9-inch pie crust
8	ounces Swiss cheese, grated
½	pound crabmeat, drained, picked over
2	green onions, sliced
3	eggs
1	cup half-and-half
¼	teaspoon lemon zest
¼	teaspoon dry mustard
½	teaspoon salt
Dash mace	

Preheat the oven to 450°F. Line the pie shell with 2 pieces of foil and bake in the oven for 8 minutes. Remove the foil and bake for 5 minutes more, until the shell is set and dry. Remove from the oven and reduce the heat to 325°F.

Sprinkle the cheese over the bottom of the shell. Top with the crabmeat and green onions. In a small mixing bowl, beat together the eggs, half-and-half, lemon, mustard, salt and mace. Pour the mixture into the crust. Cover the edges with foil and place the quiche in the oven. Bake for 40 to 45 minutes or until the eggs are set. Remove from the oven. Remove the foil and let it cool for 10 minutes before serving.

serves 8

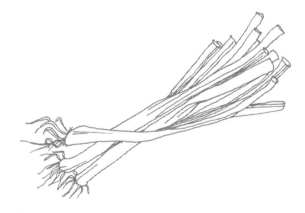

Asparagus and Crab Quiche page 70
Crab and Salmon Chowder page 57

• • •
Crab Benedict page 57

• • •
Steamed Crabs Maryland Style page 73

Carrot Blini with Crabmeat Caviar page 41
Lobster-Stuffed Tenderloin page 74

Fried Soft Shell Crabs page 91
Pesto Rounds with Shrimp page 34

Easy Apple Tart page 127, Low-Fat White Chocolate Meringue Shells page 129,
Toasted Hazelnut Chocolate Marquise page 140

Scallops Tarragon

3 mushrooms, sliced

2 green onions, sliced

2 tablespoons chopped fresh parsley

¼ cup butter

¼ teaspoon tarragon

10 sea scallops

1 cup dry white wine

In a large, heavy skillet over medium heat, sauté the mushrooms and green onions in the parsley and butter. After about 2 minutes, turn the heat to high and add the tarragon and scallops. Sauté for about 2 minutes on each side, or until the edges of the scallops begin to brown, then remove to a warm plate. Add the white wine and boil the liquid until it reduces by half.

Serve the scallops over pasta or rice and top with the sauce.

serves 2

Scalloped Oyster Crimp

1 quart select oysters

2 cups coarse cracker crumbs

Salt and freshly ground pepper to taste

¼ pound unsalted butter

¼ cup cream

Drain the oysters and then rinse in the oyster liquor. Strain and reserve the liquor. Butter a shallow oven dish; cover the bottom with a layer of cracker crumbs, then a layer of oysters. Sprinkle over the salt and pepper and dot with butter. Repeat with a second layer. Pour the oyster liquor and cream over all, covering with cracker crumbs and butter. Bake in a preheated 350°F oven for about 25 minutes.

serves 6

MENU

Brandied Blue Cheese, Walnut and Pear Crostini • 47

Bessie's Crab Pudding • 99

Fall Spinach Salad • 118

Cold Lemon Dessert • 137

Bessie's Crab Pudding

There's an Aunt Bessie in every Chesapeake Bay family, or at least a recipe for this savory casserole that finds its roots in creamy bread puddings. A genuine Eastern Shore comfort food, it's always been a favorite with my children.

6 tablespoons unsalted butter

½ cup chopped green onions

½ cup finely diced celery

1 cup chopped mushrooms

½ cup finely diced green bell pepper

1 pound crabmeat, drained, picked over

8 slices white bread, crusts removed, diced

4 eggs

2 cups milk

2 cups heavy cream

1 teaspoon salt

½ teaspoon freshly ground pepper

1 teaspoon Worcestershire sauce

Dash hot pepper sauce (such as Tabasco)

1 cup shredded sharp Cheddar cheese

In a large, heavy skillet over medium-high heat, melt the butter. Add the green onions, celery, mushrooms and green pepper and sauté until tender, about 5 to 8 minutes. Remove from the heat, gently fold in the crabmeat and set aside.

Butter a 3-quart casserole or baking dish. Place half of the diced bread on the bottom of the dish. Spread the crabmeat mixture over it and top with the remaining bread.

In a large mixing bowl using a wire whisk, beat together the eggs, milk, cream, salt, pepper, Worcestershire sauce and hot pepper sauce. Pour over the casserole, cover with aluminum foil and chill for 2 to 3 hours.

Preheat the oven to 350°F. Remove the foil from the casserole. Sprinkle with the cheese and bake for 15 minutes. Reduce the heat to 325°F and continue baking for 45 minutes. Serve hot.

serves 8 to 10

Spinach and Corn Strudel with Sauce

1 cup part-skim ricotta cheese

2 tablespoons grated Parmesan cheese

1½ cups frozen corn kernels

1 egg

½ teaspoon lemon zest

Freshly grated nutmeg or ground to taste

Salt and freshly ground pepper to taste

5 cups packed fresh spinach or 2 10-ounce packages frozen

1 tablespoon olive oil

4 sheets phyllo dough

4 tablespoons unsalted butter, melted

1½ cups fresh tomato sauce

In a medium mixing bowl, combine the ricotta, Parmesan, corn, egg, lemon zest, nutmeg, salt and pepper. Stir until well blended and set aside. If using fresh spinach, place it in a large, heavy skillet with the oil and sauté over medium heat until it wilts. Remove to a bowl and chill. If using frozen spinach, thaw and drain it well in a sieve and then place in a towel and squeeze out any excess liquid.

Brush a sheet of the phyllo dough with the butter and place another sheet on top of it. Repeat until all the sheets are used.

Preheat the oven to 400°F. With the long side of the phyllo toward you, spoon the ricotta mixture along the bottom third of the dough. Spread the spinach on top of it. Roll the phyllo up from the bottom, like a log. Tuck in the ends as you go so that the stuffing won't fall out. Place the roll on a sheet pan and bake for 20 minutes, until golden brown. Remove from the oven and let cool for a couple of minutes.

To serve, warm the tomato sauce briefly and ladle onto 4 plates. Cut 4 slightly diagonal 1-inch crosswise slices of strudel and place each one, a bit off center and cut side up, on a plate, so that the pinwheel design of the filling shows. Slice the remaining strudel into 4 pieces, each with a straight crosswise edge and a slightly diagonal edge. Stand each slice on its straight edge, like a small tower beside the strudel on the plate.

SERVES 4

Pasta with Smoked Salmon and Lemon Crème Fraîche

Crème fraîche is used in this recipe because, unlike whipping cream, it won't break down when it's heated. It adds a lovely tang that compliments the rich taste of smoked salmon in this easy-to-prepare dish.

1½   cups crème fraîche

2   tablespoons fresh lemon
      juice

2   tablespoons horseradish

1   teaspoon lemon zest

2   tablespoons unsalted
      butter

½   cup thinly sliced green
      onions

6   ounces thinly sliced
      smoked salmon

12   ounces tagliatelle or
      linguine

Salt and freshly ground
      pepper to taste

1   tablespoon chopped
      fresh chives for garnish

In a medium bowl, whisk together the crème fraîche, lemon juice, horseradish and lemon zest. Melt the butter in a large, heavy skillet over medium-high heat. Add the green onions and sauté until tender, about 3 minutes. Reduce the heat to low and add the crème fraîche mixture and the smoked salmon. Stir until heated through, about 5 minutes (do not boil). Remove from the heat.

Cook the pasta as directed in a large pot of salted, boiling water. Drain and add the pasta to the skillet with the crème fraîche. Sprinkle with the salt and pepper and toss well. Transfer to a large serving bowl and garnish with the chives.

SERVES 4

Fettuccine and Crab Carbonara

12 ounces fettuccine

½ cup grated Parmesan cheese

2 eggs, slightly beaten

2 tablespoons chopped fresh parsley

1 cup crabmeat, drained, picked over

¼ pound bacon, cooked, drained, crumbled

In a large pot of salted water, cook the pasta until *al dente*. Drain and place in a large, shallow serving bowl. Immediately add the cheese, eggs and parsley. Toss well for several minutes. This will cook the eggs slightly. Gently fold in the crabmeat. Sprinkle with the bacon and serve.

serves 4

Linguine with Crab and Vodka Sauce

2 garlic cloves, chopped

¼ cup diced ham

½ small onion, diced

1 tablespoon butter

1 cup half-and-half

1 teaspoon basil

1 tablespoon tomato paste

8 ounces linguine

½ cup crabmeat, drained, picked over

3 ounces vodka

In a medium-size skillet over medium heat, sauté the garlic, ham and onion in the butter. Cook until the vegetables are soft and the ham begins to brown. Add the rest of the ingredients, except the pasta, crab and vodka.

Bring a large pot of salted water to a boil and cook the pasta according to the manufacturer's directions. Drain and place in a serving bowl.

Heat the sauce to a gentle simmer, add the crab and vodka and cook for 1 to 2 minutes. Pour the sauce over the pasta and serve.

serves 2

Spaghetti with White Clam Sauce

Of course, prepared pasta sauces are good in a pinch when you're famished, but there's no surpassing one made from scratch. Take a little time and you'll agree the results are well worth the effort.

3	garlic cloves, mashed
1	tablespoon olive oil
2	7- or 8-ounce bottles clam juice
2	8-ounce cans minced clams
⅛	teaspoon crushed red pepper
½	teaspoon oregano
¼	cup dry white wine
1	pound spaghetti
2	tablespoons butter
¼	cup heavy cream
2	tablespoons finely chopped fresh Italian parsley

In a large, heavy skillet over medium heat, sauté the garlic in the olive oil for 3 to 5 minutes, until brown. Remove the garlic with a slotted spoon and reserve until later. Remove the skillet from the heat and add the clam juice. Drain the minced clams and add their liquid to the skillet. Mince the browned garlic and add to the clam broth. Bring to a boil and add the red pepper, oregano and wine. Lower the heat and simmer, uncovered, until the volume is reduced by half, about 20 minutes.

Cook and drain the pasta as directed on the package. Place in a large, shallow serving bowl and toss with the butter.

Stir the minced clams and heavy cream into the broth and simmer until just hot. Do not cook or the clams will toughen.

Spoon half of the clam sauce onto the pasta and toss. Sprinkle with the parsley and toss again. Top with the remaining clam sauce.

serves 4

MENU

• • •

Chorizo Puff Pastry • 42

Eastern Shore Crab Salad with Cantaloupe • 105

Mediterranean Swirl Bread • 124

Poached Pear Tart • 138

Eastern Shore Crab Salad with Cantaloupe

Red and green bell peppers sparkle in this colorful crab salad that looks tantalizing in a cantaloupe "bowl." As good as it looks, it tastes even better with hints of honey and mint, and contrasting textures of crunchy apples and peppers with soft, flavorful crab.

1	pound backfin crabmeat, drained, picked over
¼	cup diced red bell pepper
¼	cup diced green bell pepper
2	tablespoons minced green onions
¼	cup diced apple
¾	cup mayonnaise
¼	cup plain yogurt
1	tablespoon honey
2	tablespoons chopped fresh mint

Dash Worcestershire sauce

Dash hot pepper sauce (such as Tabasco)

Juice of ½ lemon

Salt and freshly ground pepper to taste

3 small ripe cantaloupe or honeydew melons, halved, seeded

Mint sprigs for garnish

Combine the crabmeat, red and green bell peppers, green onions and apple in a large bowl. In a small bowl, combine the mayonnaise, yogurt, honey, mint, Worcestershire, hot pepper sauce and lemon juice and mix well. Pour the mayonnaise mixture over the crabmeat mixture and toss gently. Season with salt and pepper.

Place each melon half, cut side up, on an individual salad plate. Divide the salad mixture evenly among the melon halves, mounding the salad in the hollow centers. Garnish with the mint springs and serve.

serves 6

Warm Goat Cheese and Crab Spinach Salad

No longer something to be hunted down in exclusive gourmet markets, good quality goat cheeses are now widely available. Happily so, for goat cheese and crab star in this salad of crisp spinach leaves tossed with a tangy tarragon mustard vinaigrette.

½	pound goat cheese
¾	cup olive oil
1	teaspoon chopped fresh thyme
1	pound spinach, washed, stems removed
1	teaspoon Dijon-style mustard
1	teaspoon chopped fresh tarragon
1½	tablespoons red wine vinegar
1	egg yolk
Salt and freshly ground pepper to taste	
2	strips bacon, cooked, drained, crumbled
½	cup crabmeat, drained, picked over

Slice the goat cheese into 8 rounds and place in a shallow bowl. Drizzle ¹/₄ cup of the olive oil and the thyme over the cheese. Cover and chill overnight.

Pat dry the spinach and tear the large leaves into pieces. Place in a large bowl.

In a small mixing bowl, using a wire whisk, combine the mustard, tarragon, red wine vinegar and egg yolk. Slowly whisk in the remaining olive oil. Add salt and pepper to taste. Pour the dressing over the spinach and toss well.

In a small, heavy skillet over a medium flame, heat 2 tablespoons of the oil from the goat cheese. Add the cheese rounds and sauté for 30 seconds on each side. Place the cheese on the spinach leaves, sprinkle with the bacon and surround with the crabmeat. Toss gently at the table or serve on individual plates.

serves 4

Chesapeake Bay Crab Salad

Be sure to find really ripe avocados to make this wonderful fresh salad. The splash of lemon juice and the sizzle of hot pepper sauce enhance the crab flavor to create a dish that's just right for a light summer luncheon.

¼ cup mayonnaise

1 teaspoon chopped pimiento

2 tablespoons Dijon-style mustard

1½ teaspoons Worcestershire sauce

½ teaspoon salt

¼ teaspoon hot pepper sauce (such as Tabasco)

2 tablespoons lemon juice

½ cup chopped celery

1 pound backfin crabmeat, drained, picked over

3 small avocados

Lettuce

Paprika

12 lemon wedges

In a large mixing bowl, combine the mayonnaise, pimiento, mustard, Worcestershire sauce, salt, hot pepper sauce, lemon juice and celery. Gently fold in the crabmeat. Chill.

Peel and halve the avocados. Remove the pits. Fill each half with the crabmeat mixture. Surround with the lettuce leaves. Sprinkle with the paprika. Serve with 2 lemon wedges on each plate.

serves 6

SIDE DISHES

Broiled Tomatoes

5   tomatoes

1   cup breadcrumbs

1   cup grated Parmesan cheese

2   tablespoons snipped fresh chives

¼   cup minced fresh parsley

1   cup butter, melted

Slice the tomatoes ¼-inch thick; discard the ends. Place them on a broiler pan. Mix the remaining ingredients and place an equal portion of the mixture on the top of each tomato. Broil for about 5 minutes or until hot and serve immediately.

serves 4

Eggplant Parmesan

Hearty and satisfying, this casserole is a faithful partner to many of my chicken dishes. My secrets for a richer flavor? Brown the eggplant slices under the broiler until the breadcrumbs are toasty, and add red and white wine to the tomato sauce.

¼ cup red wine

1 teaspoon sugar

½ cup dry white wine

1 teaspoon basil

1 teaspoon oregano

4 8-ounce cans tomato sauce

1 28-ounce can whole tomatoes, undrained, chopped

1 6-ounce can tomato paste

2 garlic cloves, minced

1 2-pound eggplant, cut crosswise in ¼-inch slices

¼ cup water

3 egg whites, lightly beaten

2 cups Italian seasoned breadcrumbs

¼ cup grated Parmesan cheese

Vegetable spray

3 cups shredded part-skim mozzarella cheese

Oregano sprigs for garnish

In a large, heavy saucepot, combine the first 9 ingredients. Bring to a boil. Lower the heat and simmer, uncovered, for 20 minutes.

Place the eggplant slices in a large bowl and cover with water. Let stand for 30 minutes. Drain well and blot dry with paper towels. In a small, shallow bowl, whisk together the ¼ cup water and the egg whites. In another shallow bowl, combine the breadcrumbs and Parmesan cheese. Coat a baking sheet with vegetable spray. Dip the eggplant, 1 slice at a time, in the egg whites and then the breadcrumbs. Place on the baking sheet.

Place the eggplant under the broiler for about 5 minutes and flip over to brown on the other side. Set aside.

Preheat the oven to 350°F. Spread half of the tomato mixture on the bottom of a 13 x 9-inch baking dish. Arrange half of the eggplant over the sauce. Top with half of the mozzarella cheese. Repeat with the remaining sauce, eggplant and cheese.

Bake for 30 minutes, until bubbly. Let stand for 5 minutes before serving. Garnish each serving with a sprig of oregano.

SERVES 8

Roasted Ratatouille

1   yellow squash

4   eggplants, sliced in half lengthwise

¼   cup olive oil

Salt and freshly ground pepper to taste

1   red bell pepper, stem and seeds removed

1   tablespoon roughly chopped fresh thyme

Preheat the oven to 450°F. Cut the squash lengthwise into ¾-inch-thick slices. Brush both sides of the eggplants and squash with olive oil and sprinkle with salt and pepper.

Arrange the eggplants and squash on a large baking pan. Cut the red pepper lengthwise into 3/4-inch slices and toss with the remaining olive oil. Sprinkle with salt and pepper and place on the baking pan with the other vegetables. Sprinkle all the vegetables with the thyme. Roast the vegetables until golden brown and tender, about 25 to 35 minutes. Remove from the oven and serve.

serves 4

Sautéed Snow Peas with Shallots

I love the iridescent green that snow peas turn when they're cooked. It's so fresh and bright! Even though it's now possible to buy this delightful pea year-round to accompany any number of fish dishes, for me it will always herald springtime.

1½ pounds snow peas

4   tablespoons unsalted butter

2   tablespoons minced shallots

½   teaspoon salt

Remove the stem and string from each snow pea. In a large, heavy skillet over medium-high heat, melt the butter. Add the snow peas and shallots and toss to coat well with the butter. Turn the heat to high and cook the snow peas, turning often, until they become bright and almost translucent, about 5 to 8 minutes. Sprinkle with the salt and serve immediately.

serves 8

Grilled Corn on the Cob with Chili Butter

Corn is a natural with crab in whatever form it's eaten, and a summer crab feast wouldn't be complete without heaping platters of sweet yellow or butter and sugar corn on the cob on every table.

½   cup butter, softened

1   teaspoon chili powder

⅛   teaspoon hot pepper sauce (such as Tabasco)

¼   teaspoon ground cumin

1   tablespoon chopped fresh cilantro

6   ears corn

Aluminum foil

3   slices bread

Place the butter, chili powder, hot pepper sauce, cumin and cilantro in a small mixing bowl. Using a rubber spatula, combine all of the ingredients. Scrape onto the end of a 10-inch piece of plastic wrap. Spread the butter out to the length of a stick of butter. Fold the short end of the plastic wrap over the butter and, holding the ends, roll into a log. Chill until firm.

Pull back the green husk, without removing it, from each ear of corn. Remove and discard the inner corn silk. Return the husk to cover the corn and wrap it in aluminum foil.

Place the bundled corn along the edges of the coals of a pit fire or atop a grill. Turn every 4 minutes and cook for 15 to 18 minutes. Remove the foil and the husk and place the corn on a serving platter.

Toast the bread slices and cut into triangles. Slice the butter log into rounds and place 1 round on each triangle of toast. Place on the platter with the corn.

serves 6

End of Summer Casserole

Farmer's market vegetables in all their seasonal glory star in this savory baked casserole that resembles a frittata. It is one of those versatile vegetable dishes that goes with almost any main course.

2	cups fresh or frozen corn kernels
3	large green bell peppers, chopped
2	medium green tomatoes, sliced
3	garlic cloves, minced
1	cup sliced green onions
1	tablespoon olive oil
1	teaspoon salt
2	teaspoons ground cumin
½	teaspoon oregano
2	teaspoons basil
¼	cup chopped fresh parsley

Freshly ground pepper to taste

Cayenne pepper to taste

1	6-ounce jar marinated artichokes
½	cup chopped black or green olives
1	small Anaheim or poblano chili, minced
½	cup grated Monterey Jack cheese
4	eggs
½	cup buttermilk

Preheat the oven to 375°F. Butter an 8 x 11-inch baking pan.

In a large skillet over medium-high heat, sauté the corn, green peppers, tomatoes, garlic and green onions in the olive oil with the salt, cumin and oregano. Cook for 8 minutes, stirring frequently. Remove from the heat. Stir in the basil, parsley, black pepper, cayenne, artichokes, olives and chili. Sprinkle the cheese over the top and fold it in until it begins to melt.

Pour the mixture into the prepared pan. In a medium-size bowl, beat the eggs and buttermilk. Pour it over the vegetables. Bake, uncovered, for 30 to 35 minutes, until bubbling.

serves 4

Sweet Potato and Pear Swirls

**SWEET POTATO
AND PEAR**

4   medium sweet
    potatoes or yams
    (2 pounds)

2   tablespoons unsalted
    butter or margarine

2   medium, ripe pears,
    peeled, halved, cored
    and chopped

¼   teaspoon ground
    cinnamon

1   egg

1   packet sweetener

PRALINE TOPPING

3   tablespoons brown
    sugar

2   tablespoons unsalted
    butter, melted

1   tablespoon half-and-
    half

⅓   cup broken pecans

For swirls: Peel and quarter sweet potatoes. Cook potatoes, covered, in a small amount of boiling lightly salted water for 25 to 35 minutes or till tender. Drain well. Melt margarine or butter in a medium skillet. Add pears, cook, covered, over medium heat till very tender, stirring occasionally. Combine potatoes, pear mixture, and cinnamon in a bowl; beat with an electric mixer on low speed. Cool slightly. With electric mixer running on low speed, beat egg into cooled mixture. Using a decorating bag with a large star tip, pipe mixture into 12 rounds (about ¹/₃ cup each) onto a greased 15 x 10 x 1 inch baking pan, building up edges slightly(or, spoon into 12 rounds on baking pan, using back of a tablespoon to make a slight indentation in center of each). Cover; chill overnight or freeze rounds till firm. (Transfer frozen potatoes to a freezer container, freeze up to 1 month.)

For topping: Stir together brown sugar, butter and half-and-half in a small mixing bowl. Stir in pecans.

To serve refrigerated rounds, drop a scant teaspoon of praline topping on each round. Bake in a 375°F oven 15 minutes or till potatoes are light brown and heated through. (To serve frozen rounds, place on a greased baking sheet drop a scant teaspoon of praline topping on each round. Bake in a 375°F oven 20 minutes or till potatoes are light brown and heated through.)

serves 12

Casserole of Red Potatoes and Tomatoes with Cheese and Rosemary

Bubbling layers of leeks, onions, potatoes, tomatoes and nutty Gruyère cheese are tantalizing when this casserole is cut and served. Equally appealing is the hint of rosemary amid the vegetables. This dish beautifully compliments chicken, fish or beef main dishes.

LEEKS

1½   tablespoons olive oil

2   cups sliced leeks (about 3 large, white and pale green parts only), washed thoroughly

1   large yellow onion

POTATOES

1¼   pounds red potatoes, unpeeled, cut into ¼-inch slices

½   teaspoon coarse salt plus more for boiling potatoes

1½   tablespoons olive oil

2   teaspoons chopped fresh rosemary

GRATIN

1   teaspoon chopped fresh rosemary

1¼   pounds ripe tomatoes, cored, cut into ¼-inch slices

1¾   cups grated Gruyère cheese

For leeks: Heat the olive oil in a medium skillet (preferably nonstick) over medium heat. Add the leeks and onion and sauté, stirring frequently, until limp and lightly browned, about 15 minutes. Spread the leeks and onion evenly in the bottom of an oiled, 2-quart, shallow gratin dish (preferably oval). Let cool.

For potatoes: In a medium saucepan, cover the potato slices with well-salted water and bring to a boil. Reduce the heat to a gentle boil and cook for 5 minutes or until the potatoes are just barely tender. Drain and rinse under cold water until cool. Pat dry. Toss the potatoes with the salt, olive oil and rosemary.

For gratin: Heat the oven to 375°F. Sprinkle ½ teaspoon of the chopped rosemary over the leeks. Starting at one end of the baking dish, lay a row of slightly overlapping tomato slices across the width of the dish. Prop the tomatoes against the dish at a 60° angle. Cover the row of tomatoes with a generous sprinkling of Gruyère. Next, arrange a row of potato slices over the tomatoes. Sprinkle again with Gruyère. Repeat with alternating rows of tomatoes and potatoes, sprinkling each with cheese and olives, until the gratin is full.

½ cup chopped black olives

½ teaspoon coarse salt

Freshly ground pepper to taste

1½ tablespoons olive oil

⅔ cup fresh breadcrumbs mixed with 2 teaspoons olive oil

Sprinkle about ½ teaspoon of salt and the remaining ½ teaspoon of rosemary over all and season with the pepper. Drizzle with the olive oil. Mix any remaining Gruyère with the breadcrumb mixture and spread this over the whole gratin. Cook until the gratin is well browned all over and the juices have bubbled for a while and reduced considerably, 60 to 65 minutes. Let cool for at least 15 minutes before serving.

serves 6 to 8 as a side dish or 4 as a main dish

Caramelized Sweet Potato Wedges

2 tablespoons unsalted butter

2 medium sweet potatoes, peeled, cut into ¼-inch wedges

1 cup water

¼ cup orange juice

¼ cup light brown sugar

Salt and freshly ground pepper to taste

In a large, heavy skillet over medium-high heat, melt the butter. Add the potato wedges and stir to coat them with the butter. Add the water and orange juice, cover and simmer gently for 5 minutes.

Remove the cover, reduce the heat to medium and continue cooking, tossing occasionally. Sprinkle the sugar over the potatoes and cook for another 10 minutes, until it becomes a brown glaze. Season with salt and pepper and serve immediately.

serves 4

Scalloped Potatoes

You won't find a dish that says comfort food faster than this one, a classic that compliments every entree—from fish to fowl to beef—that it's paired with. I like to add a layer of sliced green onions and a dash of nutmeg to enhance its old-fashioned creamy potato flavor.

6	medium potatoes
2	onions
¼	cup unsalted butter
⅓	cup sliced green onions
1	teaspoon salt
⅛	teaspoon freshly grated nutmeg or ground
¼	teaspoon freshly ground pepper
1½	cups light cream

Preheat the oven to 325°F. Peel and thinly slice the potatoes and onions. Butter a 2-quart, ovenproof casserole and place a layer of the potatoes on the bottom. Add a layer of onions, dot with butter and continue to layer in this way, ending with potatoes. Sprinkle with the green onions, salt, nutmeg and pepper. Pour the cream over the top and cover with aluminum foil.

Bake for 45 minutes. Remove the foil and bake for 30 to 40 minutes more or until the potatoes are tender and the liquid is absorbed. Turn the oven to broil and allow the top to brown, about 5 minutes.

serves 8

Crunchy Coleslaw

There are certain side dishes that have to be at a crab feast, and this is one of them. I've dressed it up a bit by adding walnuts, apples and raisins, but in any form it's a traditional Chesapeake Bay time-out food—eaten when you must take a break from eating all those crabs.

12	cups thinly sliced green cabbage
½	cup coarsely chopped walnuts, toasted
¼	cup raisins
¼	cup peeled shredded carrots
½	cup peeled diced Granny Smith apples
¼	cup diced red onion
¼	cup sour cream
¼	cup mayonnaise
2	teaspoons fresh lemon juice
2	teaspoons honey
¼	teaspoon hot pepper sauce (such as Tabasco)
½	teaspoon salt

Freshly ground pepper to taste

In a large mixing bowl, toss the cabbage, walnuts, raisins, carrots, apples and red onion. In a small mixing bowl, using a wire whisk, combine the sour cream, mayonnaise, lemon juice, honey, hot pepper sauce, salt and pepper. Pour over the cabbage, toss well and chill.

serves 6

Fall Spinach Salad

Glittering red pomegranate seeds make this salad extra festive. It's perfect for autumn entertaining and on into the holidays. The tangy citrus flavors are a natural with avocado, while toasted walnuts add intriguing texture.

3 tablespoons orange juice

3 tablespoons white wine vinegar

½ cup olive oil

2 tablespoons Dijon-style mustard

1 shallot or 3 green onions (white parts only), minced

½ teaspoon salt

¼ teaspoon freshly ground pepper

15 cups loosely packed fresh spinach leaves (about 15 ounces), torn in bite-size pieces

2 avocados, peeled, pitted, sliced

4 navel oranges, peeled, pith removed, sectioned

1 cup walnut pieces, toasted

Seeds from 1 pomegranate

To make the dressing, put the first 7 ingredients in a small bowl or a jar with a tight-fitting lid. Whisk or shake until blended.

Toss the spinach and ¹/2 cup of the dressing in a large serving bowl. Add the avocados, oranges and walnuts; toss gently to mix. Arrange on serving plates; sprinkle with the pomegranate seeds. Serve the remaining dressing on the side.

serves 12

Bacon Potato Salad

Nothing says summer like an all-American potato salad! My family loves this version at our crab feasts, and I confess that I'm always tempted to lick the spoon for another taste. This salad, with its snappy dressing and crumbled bacon, is simply outstanding with crab cakes.

2   pounds red potatoes

1   tablespoon salt

¾   cup mayonnaise

2   tablespoons stone-ground mustard

8   slices bacon, cooked, drained, crumbled

⅓   cup chopped green onions

Salt and freshly ground pepper to taste

2   tablespoons chopped fresh parsley

Quarter the potatoes and place them in a large pot. Cover with cold water, add the salt and bring to a boil. Lower the heat and simmer gently for about 20 minutes or until a potato slips off a fork when speared. Drain and place in a large mixing bowl.

In a small bowl, combine the mayonnaise and mustard. Pour over the potatoes and gently toss to coat. Sprinkle with the bacon, green onions, salt, pepper and parsley. Fold to mix. Chill before serving.

serves 6

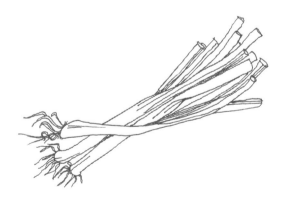

Caesar Salad

Legends abound about how Caesar salad originated, but most culinarians hail Caesar Cardini, a restaurateur in Tijuana, Mexico, as its creator. When he moved to California with his family, he brought the salad with him, and has bottled its dressing since 1948. While undercooked eggs are no longer used due to salmonella fears, this version of the dressing is just as good.

3   garlic cloves
½   cup olive oil
2   cups ½-inch bread cubes
½   teaspoon oregano
1   head romaine lettuce
½   teaspoon salt
Juice of 1 lemon
½   teaspoon Worcestershire sauce
2   eggs, boiled in their shells for 1 minute
½   cup freshly grated Parmesan cheese
4   anchovy fillets, cut into pieces

Preheat the oven to 450°F. In a medium-size mixing bowl, mash 1 clove of garlic in ¼ cup of the olive oil. Add the bread cubes and sprinkle with the oregano. Toss to coat. Place on a baking sheet and toast in the oven for 7 to 10 minutes or until they begin to brown. Using a metal spatula, turn the croutons once while they are toasting. Remove from the oven and set aside.

Wash and dry the lettuce leaves and tear into bite-size pieces. Place in a large salad bowl. In a small mixing bowl, mash the remaining 2 cloves of garlic with the salt. Stir in the remaining ¼ cup of olive oil, the lemon juice and Worcestershire sauce. Pour over the lettuce. Crack open the eggs and scoop out the inside, being careful to take out any bits of shell. Pour over the salad. Sprinkle with the cheese and toss well. Place the anchovy pieces and croutons on the top and serve on chilled plates.

serves 4

Olive Bread

If a cook's reputation is determined by her bread-making skills, this tasty bread will automatically send her to the top ranks. The fragrance of rosemary and the sparkle of Kalamata olives will awaken anyone's taste buds.

3   cups warm water

2   tablespoons or
    2 1-ounce packages
    active dry yeast

2   tablespoons olive oil

1   tablespoon salt

6   to 8 cups flour

2   cups chopped
    Kalamata olives

2   tablespoons chopped
    fresh rosemary

Place the water and yeast in a large mixing bowl and stir to mix. Let stand for about 10 minutes or until creamy and foamy. Add the olive oil and salt and mix. Add the flour, about 1 cup at a time, until you get a shaggy dough. Add the olives and rosemary and mix just until the olives are blended into the dough. Pour onto a floured board and knead until the dough is smooth and elastic. Place in a well-greased bowl and allow to rise until doubled in volume, about 1 hour.

Deflate the dough, split it into 2 pieces and form into 2 round loaves.

Preheat the oven to 400°F. Let the loaves rise for 20 to 25 minutes, then place them on a greased baking sheet and bake for about 45 minutes or until they are brown and sound hollow when tapped. Spray the oven with water for the first 5 minutes of baking time. This helps to create a nice, chewy crust. Remove from the oven and allow to cool before slicing.

makes 2 8-inch round loaves

Stuffed Rosemary Focaccia

Not only is this Italian-inspired bread delicious to eat with its tangy filling of goat cheese, olives and sun-dried tomatoes, it's also a lot of fun to make. Build its layers from the bottom up and enjoy the fragrance while it's baking. Don't be surprised when only crumbs are left.

DOUGH

1 tablespoon active dry yeast

3 cups all-purpose flour

1½ teaspoons salt

1 teaspoon coarsely ground pepper

1 teaspoon dried rosemary or 1 tablespoon fresh rosemary

¼ cup olive oil

1¼ cups water or more if needed

FILLING

Vegetable spray or vegetable oil

½ cup oil-packed sun-dried tomatoes, drained, cut into ½-inch pieces

⅓ cup Kalamata olives, pitted, cut in half

4 ounces goat cheese

2 tablespoons oil from tomatoes

Coarse salt

For dough: Place all of the ingredients in a bread machine, program for Manual or Dough and press Start. Add just enough extra water, if necessary, to make a soft, slightly tacky dough. At the end of the final knead, remove the dough from the machine to a lightly floured work space. Knead the dough several times, adding enough flour to keep it from sticking to the surface. Cover it with a clean cloth while you prepare the filling.

For filling: Spray a 9- or 10-inch springform pan with nonstick vegetable spray or coat it lightly with vegetable oil. Cut the dough in half and stretch or roll 1 of the halves to a 9- or 10-inch circle. Fit the circle into the bottom of the prepared pan. Sprinkle the dough with the tomatoes, olives, and finally, crumbles of the goat cheese, leaving a 1-inch border of dough around the circumference. Moisten the outer edge of the dough with water.

Roll the remaining dough out to a circle the same size as the first and place it over the filling. Pinch the edges of the 2 pieces of dough to close. Use the point of a knife to cut 3½-inch vent holes in the top piece of dough, cover the pan with a piece of plastic wrap and set it in a warm place to rise for 30 minutes or until doubled in bulk.

Preheat the oven to 475°F with the rack in the center position. Just before you place the pan in the oven, press down lightly with your fingertips to make indentations in the top of the dough. Drizzle on the tomato oil and sprinkle with the salt. Bake for 20 to 25 minutes or until the top is golden brown. Release the springform sides and allow the focaccia to cool for 10 minutes before cutting. Serve hot or at room temperature.

serves 8 to 10

Mediterranean Swirl Bread

Sun-dried tomatoes and spinach color the dough of this attractive loaf, while its swirled filling of sun-dried tomatoes and cream cheese is a savory surprise. I like to serve it with egg dishes for brunch, or with seafood and pasta entrées.

DOUGH

2 cups unbleached all-purpose flour

1 cup 100% whole wheat flour

¼ cup frozen spinach, thawed, squeezed in a towel to dry

2 ounces feta cheese

1 tablespoon sugar

1½ teaspoons salt

1 teaspoon regular instant yeast

1 cup water

2 tablespoons sun-dried tomatoes

FILLING

1 cup julienned sun-dried tomatoes

¼ cup sun-dried tomato oil

1 8-ounce package cream cheese or 1 cup ricotta cheese or yogurt cheese

For dough: In a large bowl, combine the flours, spinach, cheese, sugar, salt and yeast. Add the water and sun-dried tomatoes. Mix till a rough dough forms, then knead by hand for 10 minutes until a smooth dough forms. Place the dough in a greased bowl, cover and let rise till doubled in bulk, about 1 hour.

If you are using a bread machine, place all of the dough ingredients into the pan of your bread machine, program the machine for Dough or Manual, and press Start. Mix until a rough dough forms, approximately 5 to 7 minutes.

For filling: While the bread is rising, combine the tomatoes and oil in a microwave-safe bowl and microwave for 30 seconds. Stir, coating the tomatoes with oil, and let rest until cooled and soft, about 30 minutes. Place the tomatoes and oil in a food processor and process until they are finely chopped. Add the cheese, and process until fairly smooth. Set aside.

Turn the dough out onto a lightly oiled surface and allow it to rest, covered, for 10 minutes. Roll it into a rectangle about 18 x 8 inches. Spread the filling over the dough, leaving a clear inch along both the short sides and one of the long sides. Starting with the filling-covered long side, roll the dough into a log, sealing the edge and ends. Coil the log (like a snail) and place it into a greased 9-inch or 10-inch round cake pan. Cover and let it rise till doubled, about 1 hour.

Bake the bread in a preheated 425°F oven for 30 to 35 minutes, or until the interior registers 190°F to 200°F on an instant-read thermometer. Remove the bread from the oven, let it cool till you can handle it, and serve warm, in substantial slices. It's great with scrambled eggs at brunch.

makes 1 10-inch loaf

DESSERTS

Peaches and Cream Casserole

A bit like a custard and a lot like a pudding, this is an easy, fast dessert that has been in my family forever. It's a wonderful way to celebrate when the first succulent Georgia peaches arrive in the markets.

Vegetable spray

1½ cups rolled oats

1½ cups thinly sliced peeled peaches

¼ cup sugar

2 egg whites

2 teaspoons vanilla extract

¼ teaspoon almond extract

3 cups skim milk

Preheat the oven to 350°F. Lightly oil an 8-inch square baking pan or spray with vegetable spray.

In a large bowl, combine the oats, peaches and sugar. In another bowl, combine the remaining ingredients. Beat with a fork or whisk until blended. Add to the oat mixture, mixing well.

Place the mixture in the prepared pan. Bake, uncovered, for 50 minutes. Serve hot.

serves 6

Easy Apple Tart

The bounty of apples grown in Chesapeake Bay orchards never fails to astound me. Many old varieties like York and Stayman have survived in our micro-climate, while newcomers thrive as well. I love making this apple tart in autumn to celebrate their harvest.

SHORTENING CRUST

1	cup all-purpose flour
⅓	cup vegetable shortening
¼	teaspoon salt
4	tablespoons cold water

FILLING

4	small tart apples
⅓	cup sugar
½	teaspoon ground cinnamon
¼	teaspoon allspice

Pinch ground cloves

Pinch freshly grated nutmeg

1	teaspoon vanilla extract
⅓	cup dried raisins or cranberries
1	tablespoon unsalted butter, cut into small pieces

TOPPING

⅓	cup unsalted butter, softened
¼	cup sugar
3	tablespoons all-purpose flour

For crust: Place the flour, shortening and salt in a medium bowl. Mix the shortening with your fingers until it is well distributed and the mixture resembles coarse meal. Drizzle in the water while mixing the dough with a fork. Mix the dough just until it begins to come together. Wrap in plastic wrap and set aside for at least 15 minutes.

On a floured board, roll the dough out to a 12-inch disc. Fold the dough gently into quarters and then out into a 9-inch tart pan with a removable bottom. Set aside.

For filling: Place the apples, sugar, cinnamon, allspice, cloves, nutmeg, vanilla and raisins in a medium, bowl and mix well. Toss in the small pieces of butter. Spread the apple mixture over the bottom of the prepared crust and set aside.

For topping: In a small bowl, mix together the softened butter and sugar and add the flour to form a crumbly dough. Spread the topping evenly over the filling. Fold the overhanging dough over the topping all the way around the tart.

Bake the tart for 15 minutes in a preheated 425°F oven, then reduce the heat to 350°F. Bake for 20 minutes or until the tart is golden brown. Allow the tart to cool slightly and serve, still warm.

serves 8

Giant Fruit Popover

— • — • — • —

FILLING

4	tablespoons unsalted butter
1	large Granny Smith apple, peeled, cored, cut into ¼-inch slices
¼	cup sugar
¼	teaspoon ground cinnamon
¼	teaspoon ground coriander
¼	teaspoon grated fresh ginger
4	ounces dried fruit, chopped
1	tablespoon fresh lemon juice

BATTER

3	large eggs
1½	cups milk, room temperature
1½	tablespoons unsalted butter, melted
1	teaspoon vanilla extract
1⅓	cups all-purpose flour
2	tablespoons brown sugar
½	teaspoon salt
2	tablespoons confectioner's sugar

For filling: Preheat the oven to 425°F. In a medium skillet over low heat, melt the butter. Add the apple slices and sauté for 5 minutes. Add the sugar and sauté for another 5 minutes. Add the spices and cook for another few minutes, until the apples begin to brown and soften. Stir in the dried fruit and lemon juice. Pour the mixture into a pie pan.

For batter: Combine all of the ingredients except for the confectioner's sugar in a food processor or a large mixing bowl. Process or beat the mixture until smooth.

Pour the mixture over the apple filling and bake for 15 minutes at 425°F. Reduce the heat to 350°F and cook for another 20 minutes. Do not open the door or the popover, like a soufflé, may fall.

Remove from the oven, sprinkle with the confectioner's sugar and cut into wedges.

serves 8 to 10

Low-Fat White Chocolate Meringue Shells with Strawberries

3 large egg whites

½ teaspoon vanilla extract

¼ teaspoon cream of tartar

1 cup sugar

1 ounce white chocolate, grated

6 ounces reduced fat cream cheese, softened

½ cup light sour cream

2 tablespoons sugar

½ teaspoon vanilla extract

¼ cup reduced fat whipped topping

1 ounce white chocolate, chopped

½ teaspoon unsalted butter

3 to 4 cups hulled strawberries

¼ cup strawberry jam

1 to 2 teaspoons water

Let the egg whites stand in a large mixing bowl for 30 minutes. Cover a baking sheet with plain brown paper or foil and draw 8 3-inch circles. Add the vanilla and cream of tartar to the egg whites. Beat with an electric mixer on medium speed until soft peaks form (and tips curl). Add the sugar, a little at a time, beating at high speed with the mixer and scraping the sides of the bowl frequently, until stiff peaks form. Fold in the grated white chocolate into the egg whites. Spread or pipe the meringue over the circles on the paper or foil into the shape of shells.

Bake in a preheated 300°F oven for 30 minutes. Turn the oven off and let the meringue dry in the oven with the door closed for at least 1 hour. Pull off the paper and store in a closed container until ready to use. In a mixing bowl, beat together the cream cheese, sour cream, sugar and vanilla until smooth. Fold in the whipped topping. Spread evenly in the meringue shells. Cover and chill for about 1 hour. In a small saucepan, melt the chopped white chocolate with the butter. Cool. Drizzle the chocolate mixture over the top and sides of the chilled shells. Arrange the strawberries, hulled end down, over the cream cheese filling. In a small saucepan, heat the jam just until melted. Add 1 to 2 teaspoons of water to the jam and then drizzle it over the arranged berries.

serves 12

Blueberry Shortcakes

Fruit desserts mean summer to me, and a Chesapeake Bay crab feast wouldn't live up to its name without this all-American dessert. I like to serve the blueberry sauce warm so it soaks into the old-fashioned buttermilk biscuits and contrasts with the whipped cream topping.

BISCUITS

Parchment paper or short-
   ening or vegetable spray

2   cups sifted all-purpose
   flour

1   tablespoon baking
   powder, sifted to
   remove lumps

¾   teaspoon salt

3   tablespoons sugar
   plus more for glaze

1   tablespoon grated
   lemon zest

½   teaspoon freshly grated
   nutmeg or ground

4   tablespoons cold
   unsalted butter,
   cut in pieces

1   cup buttermilk plus
   more for glaze

BLUEBERRY FILLING

6   cups blueberries, picked
   over, rinsed, patted dry

For biscuits: Set a rack in the center of the oven; preheat to 400°F. Line a baking sheet with parchment or lightly grease it with shortening or vegetable spray.

In a large bowl, whisk the flour, baking powder, salt, sugar, lemon zest and nutmeg. With a pastry blender or your fingertips, cut in the butter until the mixture resembles coarse meal. Gently stir in the buttermilk until the dough just holds together with no large, dry lumps.

Spoon the dough onto the prepared baking sheet in 6 equal mounds. Brush the tops with buttermilk; sprinkle with sugar. Bake until the peaks have begun to brown and the bottoms are golden, about 20 to 25 minutes. Let rest for 1 minute and then transfer to a wire rack. While still slightly warm, slice them open with a serrated knife.

For blueberry filling: Set aside 2 cups of the berries. In a medium, nonreactive saucepan, combine the remaining 4 cups of blueberries, the sugar, water, lemon zest and nutmeg (if using). Cook, uncovered, over medium heat, stirring frequently, until very soft and juicy, 6 to 7 minutes. Remove from the heat. Taste and add lemon juice

¼   cup sugar or more
to taste

1   tablespoon water

½   teaspoon grated lemon
zest

¼   teaspoon freshly grated
nutmeg (optional)

Fresh lemon juice to taste

WHIPPED CREAM

1½   cups heavy cream,
chilled

2   tablespoons sugar

1   teaspoon vanilla extract

and more sugar, if necessary. If not using immediately, cover and refrigerate.

When ready to serve, reheat the blueberry sauce until very warm and stir in the reserved blueberries.

For whipped cream: Chill a mixing bowl and beaters for 30 minutes. In the bowl, combine the heavy cream, sugar and vanilla. Whip until medium peaks form and the beaters leave tracks on top of the cream.

Put the bottom half of each biscuit on a plate. Spoon on about ¹/₂ cup of the blueberry mixture and a few dollops of cream. Cover with the top of the biscuit. Spoon on more blueberries and top with another dollop of whipped cream. Serve immediately, passing any remaining blueberry mixture at the table.

serves 6

Flaming Rum Bananas with Meringue

Everyone loves the creamy toasted meringue and the buttery, rum-flavored bananas in this dessert. All the flavor and flair of a classic Bananas Flambé are here, but individual ramekins are much easier to serve at a dinner party.

BANANA FILLING

1   teaspoon unsalted butter

8   firm ripe medium bananas, coarsely chopped

2   tablespoons sweetener (white or brown sugar, maple syrup, honey or organic cane sugar) or to taste

5   tablespoons rum

1   tablespoon fresh lime juice or to taste

MERINGUE

5   egg whites

2   tablespoons sugar

1   teaspoon rum

½   teaspoon vanilla extract

For banana filling: Preheat the oven to 300°F. Butter 6 1-cup ramekins.

In a large sauté pan, heat the butter, and sauté the bananas for 1 minute. Stir in the sweetener and sauté for 3 to 5 minutes more, depending on the variety of banana, until the bananas are soft. Pour in the rum. Remove the pan from the heat, tilt it to catch the flambé (if you don't have a gas stove, light a match to the rum), and flambé the bananas. Simmer a few seconds, until the alcohol burns off.

Add the lime juice and adjust the seasonings, if necessary, with more sweetener or lime juice. Distribute the banana mixture evenly among the ramekins.

For meringue: Whip the egg whites until they form soft peaks. Slowly add the sugar, rum and vanilla. Whip until stiff peaks form.

Spoon the meringue on top of the banana mixture. Bake for 15 minutes, until the meringue is golden and cooked through.

serves 6

Palmiers

The French name of these small pastries is inspired by their distinctive shape which resembles the foliage of a palm tree. Crisp and sweet, they are an excellent companion to sorbets or light desserts like my Cold Lemon Dessert, page 137.

Parchment paper

1   cup sugar

12 ounces frozen puff pastry, thawed

1   egg, beaten

Preheat the oven to 400°F. Line 2 baking sheets with parchment paper. Dust a large, clean surface with some sugar. Place the puff pastry on the sugar and sprinkle it with some more sugar. Roll the pastry into a rectangle, 1/8-inch thick. Sprinkle with 1/4 cup more sugar and press the sugar into the pastry using a rolling pin.

Fold the long edges of the puff pastry into the center, so that they touch. Brush half of the pastry with some egg wash and then fold the pastry in half. Sprinkle the top with sugar and press down lightly with the rolling pin to secure the pastry.

Trim off the ends and then cut the dough crosswise into 1/2-inch slices. Place each slice, cut side up on the baking sheets, about 3 inches apart.

Place the baking sheets in the oven, reduce the heat to 375°F and cook for 8 to 10 minutes or until the bottom of the cookies begin to brown. Flip the cookies over and cook for another couple of minutes or until the other side begins to brown.

Remove from the oven and cool the cookies on a rack. Cool completely before storing.

makes 18 2-inch cookies

Crepe Napoleons with Apple Compote and Apple Caramel Sauce

Every once in a while I like to drop everything and make a dessert that's truly decadent. This one seems more difficult than it is, and the results will make you feel like a professional pastry chef. So will the raves from your dinner guests.

MASCARPONE CUSTARD

2	egg yolks
¼	cup sugar
3	tablespoons cornstarch
⅛	teaspoon salt
1½	cups half-and-half
1½	tablespoons unsalted butter
1½	teaspoons vanilla extract
8	ounces *mascarpone* cheese

APPLE COMPOTE

3	Granny Smith apples, peeled, cut into ¼-inch dice
¼	cup dried cranberries
2	tablespoons unsalted butter
½	cup brown sugar
2	tablespoons orange juice

For custard: In the insert of a double boiler, whisk together the egg yolks, sugar, cornstarch and salt. It will be very thick. Gradually whisk in the half-and-half until smooth.

Bring an inch of water to a boil in the bottom half of the double boiler. Place the insert with the egg mixture on top and cook, whisking constantly, until the mixture becomes thick, about 5 to 8 minutes. Remove the insert from the heat and stir in the butter and vanilla.

Transfer the custard to a medium bowl. Cool slightly and then whisk in the *mascarpone* until smooth. Cover with plastic wrap and chill for 2 hours.

For compote: In a medium skillet over medium heat, sauté the apples and cranberries in the butter for 5 to 8 minutes, until the apples are not quite tender. Add the brown sugar, juices and cinnamon. Simmer for another 5 minutes, until the liquid is reduced to a thick syrup.

For sauce: In a large saucepot, combine the apple juice and sugar. Bring to a boil and reduce to 2 cups. Reserve

2   teaspoons lemon juice

1   teaspoon ground
    cinnamon

APPLE CARAMEL SAUCE

1   quart apple juice

½   cup sugar

¼   cup heavy cream

1   tablespoon cornstarch

Pinch salt

½   teaspoon vanilla extract

ASSEMBLING A CREPE NAPOLEON

4   crepes (see recipe
    page 136)

Confectioner's sugar

Apple compote

Mascarpone custard

Apple caramel sauce

Mint sprig for garnish

2 tablespoons of the reduction. Lower the heat and stir in the cream. Stir and simmer for 10 minutes.

In a cup, mix the cornstarch, reserved juice and salt. Whisk into the saucepot and simmer for 2 to 4 minutes, until the sauce thickens. Stir in the vanilla extract. Pour the sauce into a bowl, cover with plastic wrap and chill.

For assembly: Preheat the oven to 400°F. Place a rack on a baking sheet. Place 4 crepes on the rack and bake them for 5 minutes or until crisp. Remove from the oven and allow to cool.

Place a crepe on a serving platter and sprinkle it with the confectioner's sugar. Spread ¼ inch of the apple compote on top of the crepe. Top with ¼ inch of the *mascarpone* custard. Add another crepe and spread with ¼ inch of custard, then compote, then a thin layer of caramel sauce. Repeat this step and top with the last crepe.

Drizzle the remaining caramel sauce over the top and garnish with a sprig of mint in the center. Cut into 6 wedges to serve.

serves 6

Basic Crepes

2 cups all-purpose flour

1 teaspoon sugar

Dash salt

1 cup club soda

1 cup 2% milk

3 eggs, slightly beaten

5 tablespoons unsalted
butter, melted

Vegetable oil

In a medium bowl, combine the flour, sugar and salt. Make a well in the center and add the club soda, milk and eggs. Whisk until smooth.

Whisk in the melted butter. Cover the bowl with plastic wrap and chill for 1 hour. Right before making the crepes, whisk again to get out any lumps.

Heat a 10-inch, stainless steel skillet over medium heat. Wipe the pan with a paper towel that has been lightly dipped in vegetable oil. Pour $1/3$ cup of the crepe batter into the pan and tip it around so that the batter spreads and coats the pan evenly. Cook the crepe until the edges brown slightly. This will take about 1 minute. Loosen the edges with a metal spatula and flip the crepe over. You can use your fingers to do this. Cook for another minute and then slide it onto a plate.

Continue to make the crepes, wiping the pan with vegetable oil as needed.

makes 12 to 15 crepes

Cold Lemon Dessert

I love the simplicity of this creamy, smooth lemon dessert. Serve it with a generous spoonful of sweet strawberries or plump blueberries and you'll have the perfect ending for a summer luncheon or dinner.

6   eggs, separated
1½ cups sugar
⅔   cup fresh lemon juice
½   cup cold water
1   tablespoon unflavored gelatin
1⅓ cups heavy cream

In the insert of a double boiler over medium heat, whisk together the egg yolks and 1 cup of sugar. Add the lemon juice and continue stirring until the custard thickens and forms a ribbon when lifted from the whisk. Remove from the heat.

Place the cold water in a small mixing bowl and sprinkle the gelatin over it. Allow it to "bloom" for 5 minutes. Place the bowl over hot water and stir until the gelatin is dissolved. Remove from the heat and stir until it returns to room temperature. Mix together the lemon custard and the gelatin.

Whip the egg whites with the remaining sugar until soft peaks are formed. Whip the cream until stiff. Fold the whipped cream into the lemon custard. Gently fold in the egg whites.

Place the dessert into a large decorative bowl or into individual cups and chill for 2 hours before serving.

serves 12

Poached Pear Tart

The fruit and almond pairing here is sensational, but be sure to use pears that are ripe to experience the full burst of flavor. With hints of cinnamon and almond in the flaky crust and an almond-flavored custard surrounding the pears, this is a grand finale for any meal.

CINNAMON CRUST

1	cup all-purpose flour
2	tablespoons confectioner's sugar
¼	teaspoon salt
¼	teaspoon ground cinnamon
½	teaspoon almond extract
4	tablespoons unsalted butter, cut into pieces

FILLING

4	pears, peeled, halved, cored
1½	cups red wine
½	cup granulated sugar
⅓	cup heavy cream
¼	cup almond paste
2	eggs
1½	teaspoons almond extract

For crust: Preheat the oven to 350°F. Place the flour, confectioner's sugar, salt, cinnamon and almond extract into a food processor fitted with a metal blade. Turn on the machine and add the butter, a piece at a time. Process until a ball of dough forms. Remove from the machine and press into a 10-inch tart pan with a removable bottom. Bake the crust for 10 minutes, until light brown. Set aside to cool.

For filling: In a medium saucepot over high heat, bring the wine and half the sugar to a boil. Add the pears and cook until the pears are fork tender, about 10 to 15 minutes. Flip the pears over a few times as they cook. Set aside and let the pears cool in the wine.

Remove the pears from the wine and cut lengthwise into 1/4-inch slices. Arrange the slices decoratively on the crust and set aside. Place the tart on a baking sheet. Freeze the wine for another use.

In a food processor, blend the cream, almond paste and remaining sugar until smooth. Add the eggs and almond extract and mix well. Pour the mixture over the pears. Bake the tart for 25 to 30 minutes or until the custard is set. Remove from the oven and cool slightly.

serves 8 to 10

Crème Caramel

Butter

1 cup sugar

3 cups half-and-half

5 eggs

¼ teaspoon salt

1 teaspoon vanilla extract

Coat the bottoms and sides of 8 6-ounce custard cups with butter. In a small, heavy skillet, over medium heat, melt ½ cup of the sugar, stirring, until it is a light brown syrup. Spoon 1 tablespoon of the syrup into each custard cup. Place the cups in a roasting pan. Preheat the oven to 350°F.

In a small, heavy saucepot over medium heat, bring the half-and-half to just a simmer. Turn off the heat. Place the eggs, the remaining ½ cup of sugar, the salt and vanilla extract in a medium-size, heatproof mixing bowl. Beat until combined well.

In another pot, bring about an inch of water to a boil. Place the bowl with the eggs over the steaming water and beat constantly with a wire whisk until they are pale yellow and hot. Gradually whisk in the half-and-half. Continue to stir until the custard begins to thicken. Pour the mixture into the custard cups.

Pour very hot water into the roasting pan holding the custard cups, up to 1 inch of their rims. Carefully place in the oven and bake for 1 hour.

Remove the custard cups from the roasting pan and allow them to cool on a wire rack. Refrigerate after they have cooled. To serve, run a knife along the sides of each custard cup and invert onto a small dessert plate, letting the syrup run down the sides.

serves 8

Toasted Hazelnut Chocolate Marquise

Chocolate lovers will swoon for this decadent dessert that marries the virtues of a sponge cake with the indulgence of a mousse. Adorned with a coffee cream sauce, its hazelnut and chocolate flavors mingle over ladyfingers to create a culinary romance.

10 ounces semisweet chocolate, finely chopped

1¼ cups heavy cream

⅔ cup superfine sugar

1 tablespoon Frangelico (hazelnut liqueur)

20 tablespoons (2½ sticks) unsalted butter, softened

½ cup unsweetened cocoa powder, sifted if lumpy

4 large egg yolks

⅓ cup ground hazelnuts, toasted

24 soft ladyfingers

3 cups heavy cream

3 tablespoons sugar

1 teaspoon instant espresso powder or more if a stronger flavor is desired

In a small bowl, melt the chocolate over a pot of steaming water. Set aside in a warm place. In a large mixing bowl, combine the 1¼ cups heavy cream, ⅓ cup of the superfine sugar and the Frangelico. Beat until the cream is frothy and slightly thick. Set aside.

In a large bowl, using an electric mixer fitted with a paddle, beat the butter and the remaining ⅓ cup of superfine sugar on medium speed until it is well blended and almost smooth. Slowly add the cocoa powder. Add the egg yolks, 1 at a time. Add the warm, melted chocolate into the cocoa mixture and beat on low speed until well blended. Scrape down the sides and bottom of the bowl. With the mixer still on low speed, gradually add the cream mixture. Stop as soon as the cream is incorporated. Sprinkle the hazelnuts over the mixture and, using a rubber spatula, gently fold them into the chocolate mixture.

Cover the bottom and sides of a 10-inch springform pan with plastic wrap. Line the bottom, in a snug, fan-like shape, with the ladyfingers facing bottom side up. Using the rubber spatula, pour the chocolate mixture over the ladyfingers. Lightly bang the entire pan against the counter to fill any gaps in the ladyfingers and to release any air bubbles. Cover the top with plastic wrap and chill overnight or up to 3 days.

In a medium saucepot, bring the 3 cups of heavy cream to a boil. Reduce the heat and simmer until it has reduced by $1/3$ and the cream is thick enough to coat the back of a spoon. This will take about 10 minutes. Remove from the heat and whisk in the sugar and espresso powder until they are dissolved. Adjust the flavor as desired. Pour into a small bowl, cover and chill until ready to serve.

When ready to serve, peel away the plastic wrap from the top. Invert the marquise on a flat serving platter. Release the springform pan and gently remove the plastic wrap. To cut into slices, dip a long, sharp knife into very hot water. Wipe it dry and immediately cut downwards between the ladyfingers. Do not lift the knife up, but rather, pull out to remove it from the marquise. Repeat the process with each cut. Serve with the coffee cream.

serves 10 to 12

High-Rise Apple Pancake

While this dessert has various names in different parts of the country—from Dutch Baby to Apple Puff Pancake—it's classic fare in Chesapeake Bay country because it can be made in a flash in just one pan, and best of all, it's kid-approved.

¼ cup margarine

6 cups peeled apple slices

¼ cup sugar

½ teaspoon ground cinnamon

½ teaspoon ground ginger

2 eggs

½ cup flour

½ cup milk

¼ teaspoon salt

1 tablespoon margarine

Strawberry preserves and maple syrup

Melt the ¼ cup margarine in a large skillet over low heat. Combine the apples, sugar, cinnamon and ginger and place in the skillet; cook until the apples are tender.

Combine the eggs, flour, milk and salt; beat until smooth. Heat an ovenproof, 8-inch skillet in a 450°F oven until it is very hot. Coat the skillet with the 1 tablespoon margarine and immediately pour in the batter. Bake on the lowest rack in the oven at 450°F for 10 minutes. Reduce the heat to 350°F and continue baking for 10 minutes or until golden brown. Top with the apple mixture and then with the preserves and syrup. Cut into wedges like a pie and serve immediately.

serves 4 to 6

Index

To order Chesapeake Bay Gourmet products call 1-800-345-1515 or visit www.qvc.com.